ELIJAH CARTER

# Hope Unshaken

*A 30-Day Devotional for Trusting God, Overcoming*
*Anxiety and Finding Strength in Hard Times*

# Contents

# 1

# Introduction

L ife has a way of shaking us.

Maybe you're in a season where uncertainty weighs heavily on your heart, where fear whispers lies, or where the future feels like an uncharted path stretching into the unknown. Perhaps anxiety has wrapped itself around your mind, convincing you that you are alone in your struggles. Maybe you've been praying for direction but feel like the heavens are silent. If so, take heart—you are not alone. And more importantly, you are not without hope.

This devotional, *Hope Unshaken*, is an invitation—a 30-day journey to strengthen your faith, quiet your anxieties, and remind you that God's promises remain firm even in the most turbulent seasons of life. This book was written for the weary, the searching, and the longing. It was created for those who need reassurance that God is still present, still working, and still holding you in His hands. No matter what you are facing, His love is unwavering, His power is limitless, and His peace is available to you even now.

## Understanding the Purpose of This Devotional

Our world is filled with uncertainty, and anxiety often takes root when we feel like we have lost control. But the truth is, we were never meant to carry the weight of life on our own. God calls us to trust in Him, to release our fears, and to rest in the certainty of His faithfulness. This devotional is here to help you do just that—one day, one prayer, one step at a time.

The words on these pages are not meant to be passively consumed, but actively lived. This devotional is not just about reading Scripture—it's about letting Scripture read you. It's about opening your heart to the transformative power of God's truth. It's about allowing Him to dismantle lies, restore what is broken, and fill the empty places within you.

Each day, you'll engage with a carefully chosen Bible verse, a devotional reflection, a guided prayer, and an action step to help you apply the message to your daily life. By the end of this journey, my prayer is that your faith will be strengthened, your anxieties lessened, and your hope unshaken.

## How to Use This Book Effectively

This book is designed as a daily companion for the next 30 days. Each devotional is structured to be read in just a few minutes, but I encourage you to go beyond just reading—meditate on the words, pray through them, and allow them to sink deeply into your heart.

- **Find a quiet space.** Whether it's early in the morning, during lunch, or before bed, set aside time to be still in God's presence. Make this a sacred appointment between you and Him.
- **Read with an open heart.** Approach each day's devotional expecting to hear from God. He speaks through His Word, and He wants to meet you where you are. His voice is often found in the stillness, so lean in and listen.
- **Engage in prayer.** Don't just read the prayer—make it your own. Pour out your worries, your hopes, and your fears before the Lord. Speak honestly, knowing that He listens with compassion and understanding.
- **Take action.** Each devotional includes a faith-building step, designed to help you apply the message practically. Faith is not just about belief—it's about living out that belief each day. Put your faith into motion, and you will begin to see God move in unexpected ways.
- **Journal your thoughts.** If possible, keep a journal nearby. Write down insights, prayers, and reflections as you go through this journey. You may be surprised at how God moves in your life over these 30 days. Your journal will serve as a testimony to His faithfulness.
- **Share with a friend.** Sometimes, faith grows stronger when we walk through challenges together. If you feel led, invite a friend or loved one to join you in this devotional journey. Encourage each other and pray for one another as you grow in trust and hope.

## *Preparing Your Heart for Transformation*

Transformation does not come from simply reading words—it comes from encountering God and allowing Him to reshape your heart. As you embark on this journey, ask the Lord to prepare you for the work He wants to do within you. Be willing to let go of control, to surrender your fears, and to trust Him with the unknown.

Some days will be easy; others may be challenging. You may come face-to-face with truths that push you out of your comfort zone. But remember this: growth happens in the stretching. Healing happens in the surrender. Strength is forged in faith. God is not looking for perfection—He is looking for a willing heart. He does not expect you to have it all together; He simply asks that you come as you are and allow Him to do the rest.

Throughout Scripture, we see how God meets His people in their struggles. He met Moses in his insecurity, David in his despair, Elijah in his exhaustion, and the disciples in their doubts. He is the same God today, and He will meet you right where you are. As you walk through these next 30 days, know that He is near. He is working in ways you cannot yet see.

As you take this step of faith, I encourage you to trust the process. God is faithful, and He will meet you in every moment. You may start this journey feeling weighed down, but I believe you will finish it with a heart that is lighter, a faith that is stronger, and a hope that is truly unshaken.

Take a deep breath. Release what you have been carrying. God is already holding it. Now, let's begin this journey together, one step at a time, as we place our trust in the One who holds all things together.

With hope and expectation,
  **Elijah Carter**

# 2

# Week 1: Trusting God in Uncertainty

L ife is filled with moments of uncertainty—seasons where the future feels unclear, and the path ahead seems hidden. But even in the unknown, God is faithful. This week, we will dive into His promises, learning how to trust in His perfect plan, lean on His strength, and find peace in knowing that He holds our lives in His hands.

# 3

# God's Promises Never Fail – (Joshua 1:9)

**S**cripture: *"Have I not commanded you? Be strong and courageous. Do not be afraid; do not be discouraged, for the Lord your God will be with you wherever you go."* – Joshua 1:9

**Devotional Reflection**

Life often feels like a journey through shifting landscapes— sometimes we walk on firm ground, full of confidence and certainty, and other times we find ourselves standing at the edge of the unknown, afraid to take the next step. We long for stability, yet the world around us is filled with change. Plans fall apart, relationships shift, and unexpected challenges arise. In these moments, it's easy to wonder: *Is God really with me? Will He come through for me this time?*

Joshua must have asked himself similar questions as he stood before the vast and uncertain future that awaited him. He had spent years following Moses, watching God perform miracles—parting the Red Sea, providing manna in the wilderness, leading His people with a cloud by day and fire by night. But now, Moses was gone, and Joshua had been chosen to lead the Israelites into the Promised Land. The weight of this responsibility must have felt overwhelming. Would he be strong enough? Would God truly go with him as He had with Moses?

In the midst of Joshua's uncertainty, God spoke. But He didn't offer mere encouragement—He gave a command: *"Be strong and courageous."* Not once, but multiple times, God reinforced this call. Strength and courage weren't just emotions Joshua needed to muster up; they were a response to an unshakable truth: *"The Lord your God will be with you wherever you go."*

God wasn't telling Joshua to be fearless because there was nothing to fear. He wasn't promising that the journey would be easy. Instead, He was reminding Joshua that no matter what lay ahead, *His presence would never leave him.* The battles would come, the challenges would arise, but Joshua would not face them alone. The same God who had delivered Israel from Egypt, who had sustained them in the wilderness, was the same God who would walk beside him into this new and uncertain season.

Maybe today, you find yourself standing in Joshua's shoes—facing the unknown, feeling the weight of responsibility, wondering if you have the strength to keep moving forward. Fear may be whispering that you are not capable, that the future is too uncertain, that the road ahead is too difficult. But just as

He did with Joshua, God speaks into your heart: *Be strong. Be courageous. Do not be afraid. I am with you.*

This promise is not just for Joshua—it is for you. It is for every moment of doubt, every anxious thought, every uncertain step. It is a reminder that God's faithfulness does not expire, His presence does not waver, and His promises do not fail. The same God who guided Joshua into the Promised Land is guiding you today.

Yet, the enemy will try to make you believe otherwise. He will plant seeds of doubt, whispering that you are alone, that your circumstances are too difficult, that God has forgotten you. But truth stands against these lies: *God is with you. He has commanded you to be strong, not because of your own ability, but because of His unwavering presence.*

There is no season of life that His promises do not cover. Whether you are stepping into something new, facing an overwhelming challenge, or simply struggling to trust, His Word remains true: *He will never leave you nor forsake you.* When uncertainty threatens to shake your faith, stand firm on this unchanging truth.

What situation in your life today requires courage? Where do you need to be reminded that God is with you? His promise is not just a comforting thought—it is a reality. He walks with you through every valley, stands beside you in every battle, and leads you forward with strength that does not come from yourself, but from Him.

Take heart. Lift your eyes. God's promises never fail.

## Prayer

Heavenly Father, thank You for the reassurance of Your presence. In times of uncertainty, when fear and doubt creep in, remind me that You are with me. Help me to be strong and courageous, not because of my own strength, but because of who You are. When I face the unknown, let me stand firm in Your promises, trusting that You will guide me every step of the way. Fill my heart with faith and peace, and let me walk in the confidence that You are always by my side. In Jesus' name, Amen.

## Faith-Building Action Step

Take a moment to reflect on a situation where you feel anxious or uncertain. Write down Joshua 1:9 and place it somewhere visible—a sticky note on your mirror, a reminder on your phone, or a note in your journal. Every time you see it, speak it aloud and declare God's promise over your life. Choose today to trust that He is with you, wherever you go.

# 4

# Letting Go of Fear – (Isaiah 41:10)

**S**cripture: *"So do not fear, for I am with you; do not be dismayed, for I am your God. I will strengthen you and help you; I will uphold you with my righteous right hand."* – Isaiah 41:10

**Devotional Reflection**

Fear is one of the most powerful emotions we experience. It can grip our hearts, cloud our judgment, and hold us back from stepping into the life God has called us to live. Whether it's fear of failure, fear of the unknown, fear of rejection, or fear of losing control, it often paralyzes us, keeping us stuck in a place of worry and hesitation.

But God never intended for fear to have a hold over us. Throughout Scripture, He tells His people again and again, *"Do not fear."* Not because life will be free of challenges, but because He is with us. Isaiah 41:10 is one of the most reassuring promises in the Bible, a direct command from God Himself:

*"Do not fear, for I am with you; do not be dismayed, for I am your God."*

These words were spoken to the Israelites at a time when they were feeling weak, vulnerable, and unsure of the future. They had been through trials, and more lay ahead. But in the face of their fear, God reminded them that His presence was their source of strength. He didn't promise them an easy path, but He did promise to be with them every step of the way.

Maybe today, fear is weighing heavy on your heart. Perhaps you're facing an uncertain future, carrying burdens that feel too big to bear. Maybe your thoughts are filled with worry about things you can't control—your finances, your health, your family, your purpose. Fear has a way of whispering lies: *What if things don't work out? What if I'm not strong enough? What if I fail?*

But God speaks a different truth. *"Do not fear, for I am with you."* The presence of fear does not mean the absence of faith, but it does mean that we have a choice to make: Will we trust in our own strength, or will we lean into the strength of the One who holds us in His righteous right hand?

When God says, *"Do not be dismayed, for I am your God,"* He is reminding us of His authority. He is not just any god—He is *our* God. The One who created the heavens and the earth, who commands the seas and calls the stars by name, is the same God who is personally invested in our lives. He does not leave us to fend for ourselves. He is not distant. He is present. He is working in ways we cannot see, orchestrating things for our good.

Fear tells us to shrink back, but God calls us to step forward in faith. He doesn't ask us to be fearless on our own. He doesn't tell us to muster up courage from within ourselves. Instead, He says, *"I will strengthen you and help you; I will uphold you with my righteous right hand."* This is not a passive promise—it is active. God is moving on our behalf. He strengthens us when we feel weak. He helps us when we feel helpless. He upholds us when we feel like we are falling apart.

Think about what happens when a small child stumbles while learning to walk. A loving parent doesn't scold them for being weak. Instead, they reach out, steady them, and help them take another step. That is the picture of God's promise to us. When we feel like we are falling, He is already holding us up. When we feel like we can't take another step, He is right there, helping us move forward.

So how do we let go of fear? It starts by shifting our focus. Fear magnifies the problem, but faith magnifies God. When we fix our eyes on Him—when we remind ourselves of His promises, His faithfulness, His presence—fear loses its grip. Fear thrives in uncertainty, but when we trust that God is in control, uncertainty turns into an opportunity to depend on Him more deeply.

Letting go of fear is not a one-time decision; it's a daily surrender. Each morning, we have the choice to hold onto our fears or to hand them over to God. Each time anxiety rises, we have the choice to dwell on it or to replace it with His truth.

And every time we feel overwhelmed, we have the choice to remind ourselves that we are not alone.

God is with you today. He is with you in the quiet moments and in the chaotic ones. He is with you in your doubts and in your breakthroughs. He sees the fears you carry, and He gently whispers: *You don't have to hold onto that anymore. I am here.*

Take a deep breath. Release what you've been clinging to. Rest in the assurance that He is upholding you with His righteous right hand. Fear has no place where faith in God's presence remains.

**Prayer**

Father, I come before You today with the fears that weigh on my heart. You see them all. You know my worries, my doubts, and the thoughts that keep me up at night. But You have told me not to fear, because You are with me. You have promised to strengthen me, to help me, to uphold me when I feel weak.

Lord, I choose today to trust You more than my fears. I choose to believe that Your presence is enough. Remind me that You are bigger than any obstacle, more powerful than any uncertainty, and closer than I can imagine. Fill my heart with peace that comes from knowing You are in control. Thank You for being my refuge, my strength, and my constant help. In Jesus' name, Amen.

**Faith-Building Action Step**

Find a quiet place today, free of distractions, and take a few minutes to talk to God about the fears that have been weighing on your heart. Speak Isaiah 41:10 out loud as a declaration over your life. Then, write down one specific fear you are surrendering to God today. As you do, remind yourself that you are not alone—God is with you, and He is holding you in His righteous right hand.

# 5

# Faith Over Feelings – (2 Corinthians 5:7)

S **cripture:** *"For we walk by faith, not by sight."* – 2 Corinthians 5:7

**Devotional Reflection**

Feelings are powerful. They can uplift us or bring us down, inspire us to take bold steps or paralyze us with fear. They shape the way we see the world, the way we respond to situations, and even the way we perceive God. Some days, faith feels easy—when life is going well, prayers are answered, and peace seems abundant. But what happens when doubt creeps in? When prayers seem to go unanswered? When discouragement settles in like a heavy fog?

Faith was never meant to be dependent on how we feel. Paul reminds us in 2 Corinthians 5:7 that we are called to walk by faith, not by sight. This means that faith is not about what we see, what we feel, or what seems logical in the moment—it's about trusting in God's promises, even when our emotions tell us otherwise.

There will be times when faith feels distant, when you don't "feel" God's presence, when worry seems louder than truth. But faith is not measured by emotions—it is measured by trust. If we only believe God is working when we feel it, our faith will be inconsistent, wavering with every change in circumstances. But when we choose to trust God beyond what we feel, we step into a deeper and more unshakable faith.

Think about Peter when he stepped out of the boat to walk on water. As long as his eyes were fixed on Jesus, he was able to walk on the waves. But the moment he allowed fear to dictate his actions—when he looked at the wind and the waves instead of at Jesus—he began to sink. His faith wavered because he trusted in what he saw and felt, rather than in who Jesus was.

How often do we do the same? We step out in faith, but then we let fear, discouragement, or uncertainty pull us under. We allow our emotions to define our reality instead of holding onto God's truth. When we don't feel His presence, we assume He has left us. When things don't go as expected, we think He has abandoned us. When we don't receive immediate answers, we believe He isn't listening. But none of these thoughts reflect the truth of who God is. He is constant. He is present. He is working, even when we can't see or feel it.

Faith is not about ignoring our emotions or pretending they don't exist. God created us with emotions, and He understands them fully. Even Jesus, during His time on earth, experienced

17

the full range of human emotions—grief, sorrow, joy, anger, compassion. But Jesus never allowed His feelings to dictate His faith. In the Garden of Gethsemane, as He faced the suffering of the cross, He was overwhelmed with sorrow. He even prayed, *"Father, if You are willing, take this cup from Me; yet not My will, but Yours be done."* (Luke 22:42). In that moment, His emotions were heavy, but His faith remained firm. He trusted the Father's plan, even when it was difficult.

This is the kind of faith we are called to have—a faith that remains steady, even when emotions fluctuate. A faith that says, *"I trust You, God, even when I don't understand."* A faith that stands firm, not because we always feel strong, but because we know that God is strong.

Feelings will come and go. One day, you might wake up with a sense of peace and joy, confident in God's goodness. The next, you may feel anxious, overwhelmed, or uncertain. But God has not changed. His promises are just as true on the hard days as they are on the easy ones.

When doubts arise, remind yourself that your faith is not based on emotions—it is based on God's truth. When fear whispers that God is distant, choose to believe that He is near. When discouragement tells you that your prayers don't matter, hold onto the promise that He hears you. When your heart feels weary, trust that He is still working.

Walking by faith means surrendering the need to always understand. It means trusting that God is good, even when life feels uncertain. It means choosing to believe that He is in control, even when circumstances seem chaotic. It means stepping forward, even when we don't know what the next step will bring.

Faith is not a feeling—it is a choice. A choice to trust. A choice to believe. A choice to stand on the unchanging Word of God, rather than the ever-shifting emotions of the moment.

Where in your life are you allowing feelings to dictate your faith? Where is God calling you to trust Him more deeply? He is not asking you to ignore your emotions, but He is asking you to put your faith in something greater. His promises. His presence. His never-failing love.

You may not always feel strong, but God is your strength. You may not always feel His presence, but He is always with you. You may not always understand, but He is always faithful. Keep walking. Keep believing. Keep trusting. He will never fail you.

**Prayer**

Father, I thank You that my faith is not dependent on my feelings, but on Your unchanging truth. There are moments when I feel distant from You, when doubt creeps in, and fear tries to take over. But You have called me to walk by faith, not by sight. Help me to trust You, even when I don't understand.

When my emotions try to overwhelm me, remind me of Your promises. When I feel uncertain, strengthen my heart. Let my faith be rooted in who You are, not in what I see or feel. Teach me to rely on Your truth above all else. I choose today to walk in faith, believing that You are with me, guiding me, and working in ways I cannot see. In Jesus' name, Amen.

## Faith-Building Action Step

Take a moment to reflect on an area in your life where you have been relying on your emotions rather than on faith. Write down one truth from Scripture that speaks to this area, and place it somewhere you will see it daily. Each time you feel doubt creeping in, speak that truth aloud and remind yourself that your faith is grounded in God's Word, not in how you feel in the moment.

# 6

# Finding Rest in God – (Matthew 11:28)

**S**cripture: *"Come to me, all you who are weary and burdened, and I will give you rest."* – Matthew 11:28

**Devotional Reflection**

Weariness is a weight the soul was never meant to carry alone. Life has a way of pressing down on us, demanding more than we feel we can give. There are seasons when exhaustion is more than physical—it seeps into our hearts, our minds, and our spirits. We carry worries that don't seem to fade, burdens that feel too heavy to bear. Some days, we try to push through, telling ourselves to be strong. Other days, we feel like collapsing under the weight of it all.

Jesus sees this weariness. He knows how the burdens of life can feel overwhelming. He knows how exhaustion, whether from stress, pain, grief, or uncertainty, can drain us. And He offers an invitation unlike any other: *"Come to me, all you who are weary and burdened, and I will give you rest."*

It is not a conditional invitation. Jesus does not say, *Come to me when you have it all figured out.* He does not say, *Come to me only when you feel strong enough.* He simply says, *Come.* Bring your burdens. Bring your exhaustion. Bring the weight you have been carrying for far too long. He does not expect you to fix yourself first. He simply calls you to step into His presence and receive the rest that only He can provide.

Rest is not just about physical stillness. It is about the deep, soul-refreshing peace that comes from trusting that God is in control. It is a rest that silences the voice of worry and replaces it with the assurance of His care. It is the kind of rest that settles the heart, reminding it that it doesn't have to strive to earn God's love—it is already freely given.

But many of us resist this rest. We convince ourselves that we have to keep going, keep striving, keep fixing everything on our own. We carry burdens that were never meant to be ours. We cling to worries, replaying them over and over in our minds, as if we can somehow solve them by thinking about them enough. We hesitate to lay them at Jesus' feet, fearing that if we let go, we might lose control.

Yet Jesus does not call us to a life of endless striving. He calls us to Himself. He invites us to exchange our weariness for His peace, our burdens for His rest. He does not promise that life will be free from challenges, but He does promise that we do not have to face them alone.

Imagine a child who has spent the day running, playing, and expending every ounce of energy they have. By evening, they are exhausted, barely able to keep their eyes open. They don't analyze their fatigue or try to push through it—they simply climb into the arms of a loving parent and rest. They trust that they are safe, that they are cared for, that they don't have to hold themselves up any longer.

This is the kind of rest Jesus offers. A rest that does not depend on circumstances but on trust. A rest that allows you to release what you have been holding onto and simply *be* in His presence.

When Jesus says, *"I will give you rest,"* He is making a promise. He is offering something the world cannot give. The world tells us that rest comes from fixing all our problems, from achieving more, from finding solutions on our own. But true rest is not found in circumstances—it is found in Him.

If you are feeling weary today, if the weight of life feels too heavy, hear His invitation again: *Come to me.* There is no expectation for you to carry it all. There is no requirement to have everything figured out. He is not asking for perfection. He is simply asking for surrender.

What would it look like to truly rest in God? To hand over the burdens you have been carrying and trust that He is strong enough to carry them for you? It may not come naturally at first. Surrendering our worries can feel unfamiliar, especially when we have spent so much time holding onto them. But each time we choose to trust, each time we release our fears into His hands, we are learning to walk in the rest that He so freely gives.

God's rest is not an escape from reality—it is a deeper aware-ness of His presence in the midst of it. It is knowing that He is working, even when we cannot see. It is believing that His grace is sufficient, even when we feel weak. It is choosing to let go, not because we have given up, but because we trust that He is in control.

You do not have to carry this burden alone. You do not have to keep running on empty. Jesus is here, inviting you into His rest. Will you take Him at His word?

Close your eyes for a moment. Breathe deeply. Release what you have been holding onto. And hear His voice saying, *Come to me, and I will give you rest.*

## Prayer

Lord, I come to You today with the burdens I have been carrying. You see my exhaustion, my worries, and my fears. You know the weight that has been pressing down on my heart. And yet, You offer me rest—not just a momentary relief, but a deep, abiding peace that comes from trusting You.

Help me to surrender the things I cannot control. Teach me to release my worries into Your hands. When I am tempted to strive and fix everything on my own, remind me that You are already at work. Let me rest in the assurance that You are holding me, that I am not alone, and that Your love is enough.

Fill my heart with the peace that only You can give. Let Your presence be my refuge, my strength, and my rest. I choose today to come to You, to lay my burdens down, and to trust that You will carry me through. In Jesus' name, Amen.

**Faith-Building Action Step**

Set aside time today to rest in God's presence. Find a quiet place, free from distractions, and bring your worries before Him. As you pray, physically open your hands as a sign of surrender, releasing what you have been holding onto. Allow yourself to breathe deeply, resting in the truth that God is with you, and that His rest is yours to receive.

# 7

# When God Feels Distant – (Psalm 34:18)

**S**cripture: *"The Lord is close to the brokenhearted and saves those who are crushed in spirit."* – Psalm 34:18

## Devotional Reflection

There are moments in life when God feels distant—when prayers seem to go unheard, when silence stretches longer than we expected, when the presence we once felt so strongly now feels out of reach. In these seasons, doubt can creep in like a shadow, whispering that maybe God has forgotten us, or worse, that He was never truly there at all.

Faith is easy when we can feel God's nearness, when His presence feels tangible in our everyday moments. But what happens when we don't feel Him? When the warmth of His presence is replaced by what seems like emptiness? The silence can be unsettling, making us question everything we thought we knew.

If you have ever felt this way, you are not alone. Some of the greatest figures in Scripture have walked through the same experience. David, a man after God's own heart, wrote many Psalms crying out in distress, asking where God was in his pain. *"How long, Lord? Will you forget me forever? How long will you hide your face from me?"* (Psalm 13:1). Even Jesus, in His most agonizing moment on the cross, cried out, *"My God, my God, why have You forsaken me?"* (Matthew 27:46).

It is comforting to know that feeling distant from God does not mean something is wrong with our faith. It does not mean we have failed, or that God has withdrawn His love. It means we are human. Our emotions, our circumstances, and the struggles we face can make it harder for us to sense His presence—but that does not mean He is not there.

Psalm 34:18 reminds us of a powerful truth: *"The Lord is close to the brokenhearted and saves those who are crushed in spirit."* Notice that this verse does not say, *"The Lord becomes close when you feel Him."* It says that He *is* close. His nearness is not dictated by our emotions. It is a truth that remains, whether we can perceive it or not.

Perhaps today, you find yourself feeling spiritually dry, longing to hear from God but met with silence. Maybe you have been praying for answers, only to feel like you are speaking into the void. Maybe your heart is burdened with sorrow, and in the depths of your pain, God seems far away. But hear this: **He is near.**

He is near in the quiet, in the waiting, in the moments where faith feels fragile. He is near when your heart aches with disappointment, when your prayers feel weak, when you wonder if He is listening at all. Even when you cannot feel Him, He is holding you closer than you realize.

Think about a cloudy day, when the sun is hidden behind thick layers of gray. Though you cannot see it, the sun has not disappeared—it remains just as present as ever, shining above the clouds, unaffected by what we can or cannot perceive. God's presence is the same. The clouds of hardship, grief, or spiritual dryness may make it difficult to sense Him, but He is there, steady and unchanging.

In these moments, we must learn to trust His character over our feelings. God has promised that He will never leave us nor forsake us (Deuteronomy 31:6). He does not abandon His children. Even in the silence, He is working. Even when we cannot feel Him, He is guiding. Sometimes, He speaks in whispers rather than shouts. Sometimes, He is teaching us to lean in, to seek Him more deeply, to trust that His presence is not dependent on our emotions but on His eternal faithfulness.

The enemy would love nothing more than for us to mistake silence for absence. He wants us to believe that if we do not feel God, then He must not be there. But faith is believing that even when we do not see, even when we do not feel, even when we do not understand—God is present. He is near to the brokenhearted. He saves those who are crushed in spirit.

When you find yourself struggling to sense God's nearness, hold onto His promises. Speak them over your life. Remind yourself of who He is, even when your emotions try to tell you otherwise. Keep seeking Him, even when it feels hard. Keep praying, even when the words feel empty. Keep trusting, even when the silence lingers.

God is not distant. He is closer than you think. In your pain, He is near. In your questions, He is near. In your waiting, He is near. Rest in the truth that His love has never left you, and it never will.

## Prayer

Father, I come before You today with a heart that longs to feel Your presence. There are moments when You seem far away, when my prayers seem to go unanswered, and my heart grows weary in the waiting. But Your Word tells me that You are close to the brokenhearted, that You save those who are crushed in spirit.

Help me to trust this truth, even when my feelings tell me otherwise. Remind me that Your presence is not dependent on what I see or feel, but on who You are. Give me faith to believe that You are near, even in the silence. Strengthen me in the moments when doubt creeps in, and let me find comfort in knowing that You are always at work in ways I cannot see.

I surrender my need to always feel in control. I choose to rest in Your promises, knowing that You have never abandoned me and never will. Thank You for being a God who stays, a God who holds me close, a God who is faithful through every season. In Jesus' name, Amen.

## Faith-Building Action Step

Find a quiet place today, and spend a few moments in stillness before God. Even if you don't feel His presence, choose to believe that He is with you. Write down Psalm 34:18 and keep it close as a reminder that God is near, even in the moments when He feels distant. Whenever doubt tries to take hold, speak this truth aloud and declare His nearness over your life.

8

# Choosing Faith in the Storm – (Mark 4:39-40)

S **cripture:** *"He got up, rebuked the wind and said to the waves, 'Quiet! Be still!' Then the wind died down and it was completely calm. He said to His disciples, 'Why are you so afraid? Do you still have no faith?'"* – Mark 4:39-40

## Devotional Reflection

Storms have a way of revealing what we truly believe. When the skies are clear and life is calm, it is easy to say we trust God. But when the winds rise, when uncertainty rages, when we are caught in the middle of something we cannot control—this is where faith is tested.

The disciples knew what it was like to be caught in a storm. They had spent the day with Jesus, witnessing His miracles, listening to His teachings, and seeing firsthand the power He carried. But then came the night, and with it, a storm unlike any they had faced before. The wind howled, the waves crashed over the boat, and the water rose higher, threatening to sink them. Fear took hold.

And Jesus? He was asleep.

To the disciples, this must have felt unthinkable. How could He sleep while they were struggling to survive? Did He not see what was happening? Did He not care? They rushed to Him, shaking Him awake, their voices filled with panic: *"Teacher, don't You care if we drown?"* (Mark 4:38).

How many times have we felt the same? When storms arise in our lives—when the bad news comes, when the job is lost, when the relationship crumbles, when the future feels uncertain— it can seem as though God is silent, distant, unaware of our struggle. We cry out, *God, don't You see what I'm going through? Don't You care?*

And just as He did that night on the sea, Jesus rises and speaks: *"Quiet! Be still!"* With a word, the wind stops. The waves settle. The storm is no more.

Then He turns to His disciples and asks a question that must have lingered in their hearts long after the sea was calm: *"Why are you so afraid? Do you still have no faith?"*

Jesus was not rebuking them for feeling afraid; fear is a natural response to the unknown. But He was calling them to something greater—to a faith that remains steady even in the storm. The disciples had seen His power, heard His words, and walked with Him daily, yet in the moment of crisis, their fear overshadowed their faith.

How often do we do the same? We believe in God's goodness when life is going well, but when hardship comes, we panic. We let fear take the lead, forgetting the One who is in the boat with us. The storm may be raging, but Jesus is present. And if He is in the boat, then we are never truly in danger.

Faith in the storm is not about pretending the waves aren't real. It is about remembering who is greater. It is about choosing to believe that the One who commands the wind and the waves is the same One holding your life in His hands.

Maybe today, you are facing a storm of your own. Perhaps it is an unexpected hardship, a season of uncertainty, a situation that feels too big for you to handle. The waves are rising, and fear is whispering that you won't make it through. But hear the voice of Jesus, steady and unwavering: *"Why are you so afraid? Do you still have no faith?"*

This is not a question of condemnation—it is an invitation. An invitation to trust, to let go of fear, to believe that God is in control even when everything around you feels uncertain. The storm may be strong, but He is stronger.

Faith does not mean the storm disappears instantly. Sometimes, God calms the storm around us; other times, He calms the storm within us. Either way, His presence is our anchor.

So, what does it look like to choose faith in the storm? It means refusing to let fear have the final say. It means standing firm in the promises of God, even when circumstances try to shake you. It means fixing your eyes on Jesus rather than on the waves.

The disciples were never in real danger—not because the storm wasn't fierce, but because Jesus was with them. And the same is true for you.

The storm will not sink you. The waves will not overtake you. The wind will not break you. Because the One who speaks *"Peace, be still"* is still in control.

**Prayer**

Father, I come to You today with the storms in my life. You see the struggles I am facing, the worries that try to take hold of my heart. When fear rises, remind me that You are in control. When the waves feel too strong, help me to fix my eyes on You rather than on my circumstances.

Lord, I choose to trust You, even when I don't understand. I choose to believe that You are greater than any storm I face. Fill my heart with peace that goes beyond what I can see. Let Your presence be my refuge, my strength, my steady anchor in the middle of the chaos.

Thank You for being with me always. Thank You for being a God who speaks peace into the storms of life. Help me to walk by faith, not by fear. In Jesus' name, Amen.

**Faith-Building Action Step**

Think about a current challenge in your life that feels overwhelming. Take a moment to pray and surrender it to God. Speak Mark 4:39-40 over your situation, declaring that Jesus is in control. Write down one truth about God's power that you will hold onto this week as a reminder that He is greater than the storm.

# 9

# Praying Through Doubt – (Philippians 4:6-7)

**S**cripture: *"Do not be anxious about anything, but in every situation, by prayer and petition, with thanksgiving, present your requests to God. And the peace of God, which transcends all understanding, will guard your hearts and your minds in Christ Jesus."* – Philippians 4:6-7

**Devotional Reflection**

Doubt has a way of creeping into our hearts when we least expect it. It often begins as a quiet whisper—*What if God isn't really listening? What if things don't work out? What if my prayers don't make a difference?* Over time, that whisper can grow louder, filling our minds with uncertainty and weighing heavy on our spirits.

Faith and doubt can coexist. Many of the greatest men and women in Scripture wrestled with uncertainty. Abraham questioned how God would fulfill His promise. Moses doubted his ability to lead. Even John the Baptist, after proclaiming Jesus as the Messiah, sent a message from prison asking, *"Are You the one who is to come, or should we expect someone else?"* (Matthew 11:3).

Doubt does not disqualify us from faith. It is a human response to the unknown, a reaction to the moments when life does not go as expected. But what we do with our doubt matters. When doubt rises, we have a choice: we can allow it to pull us away from God, or we can bring it to Him in prayer.

Paul's words in Philippians 4:6-7 offer a powerful invitation: *Do not be anxious about anything, but in every situation, by prayer and petition, with thanksgiving, present your requests to God.* This is not just a command to stop worrying—it is a call to shift our focus. Instead of being consumed by doubt, we are called to bring everything to God in prayer.

Prayer is not about having the perfect words or always feeling strong in our faith. It is about honesty. It is about coming before God as we are—uncertain, struggling, full of questions— and choosing to trust that He hears us.

When we pray through doubt, we are not ignoring our questions or pretending they don't exist. We are surrendering them. We are laying them at the feet of the One who sees the full picture, the One who understands what we cannot. We are choosing to trust that even when we don't have all the answers, God is still good.

Paul does not promise that prayer will always bring immediate answers. But he does promise that when we present our requests to God, something miraculous happens: *The peace of God, which transcends all understanding, will guard your hearts and your minds in Christ Jesus.*

This peace is not the kind that comes from circumstances being resolved exactly as we hope. It is a supernatural peace, one that does not make sense in the midst of uncertainty. It is the kind of peace that allows us to breathe deeply even when we don't know what comes next. It is the kind of peace that quiets the voice of fear and reminds us that we are held by a God who never lets go.

Maybe today, you are struggling with doubt. Maybe you have been praying for something, but the answer has not come. Maybe you are wondering if God hears you, if He cares, if your prayers truly matter. The enemy would love for you to believe that your doubts mean you are alone, that you have to figure things out on your own. But God invites you to something different. He invites you to bring it all to Him—to pour out your heart, your fears, your questions—and to allow His peace to guard you.

Praying through doubt is an act of trust. It is choosing to turn to God rather than away from Him. It is standing in faith, not because we always feel certain, but because we believe that He is faithful.

God is not intimidated by your doubts. He does not turn away when you question or struggle. Instead, He draws near. He listens. He holds you in His hands and whispers, *I am here. Keep trusting. Keep praying. I am working in ways you cannot yet see.*

Let prayer be your refuge. Let it be the place where doubt is exchanged for faith, where anxiety is met with peace, where fear is quieted by the assurance that God is always in control.

## Prayer

Father, I come before You today with the doubts and worries that have been weighing on my heart. There are moments when I struggle to understand, when I question how You are working in my life. But Your Word tells me not to be anxious, but to bring everything to You in prayer.

So today, I lay it all at Your feet. My questions, my uncertainties, my fears—I surrender them to You. I ask that You replace my doubt with faith, my anxiety with peace. Help me to trust in Your goodness, even when I don't see the full picture. Remind me that You are always working, always present, always faithful.

Fill my heart with the peace that surpasses understanding. Guard my mind against fear. Let my soul find rest in the truth that You are in control. Thank You for being a God who listens, who cares, and who never leaves me alone in my struggles. I trust You, Lord. In Jesus' name, Amen.

## Faith-Building Action Step

Set aside time today to bring your doubts to God in prayer. Be honest about what is weighing on your heart. Write down

Philippians 4:6-7 as a reminder that God invites you to bring everything to Him. Each time worry or doubt tries to take hold, pray and release it to Him, trusting that His peace will guard your heart and mind.

# 10

# Week 2: Overcoming Anxiety & Fear

F ear and anxiety can feel overwhelming, but they were never meant to define you. God calls you to a life of peace, not panic, of trust, not turmoil. This week, we will explore how to cast our cares upon Him, embrace His perfect peace, and walk forward in faith, knowing that He is always with us.

# 11

# Cast Your Cares on Him – (1 Peter 5:7)

**S**cripture: *"Cast all your anxiety on Him because He cares for you."* – 1 Peter 5:7

**Devotional Reflection**

Anxiety has a way of creeping into the corners of our minds, whispering doubts and fears that take root and grow if left unchecked. It often starts small—a single thought of worry, a fleeting concern about the future—but before long, it can feel like a heavy burden pressing down on our hearts. The weight of uncertainty, stress, and fear can make it difficult to move forward, leaving us feeling stuck in a cycle of worry.

We try to carry these burdens on our own, thinking that if we just try a little harder, if we just plan a little better, if we just control every possible outcome, maybe then we will find peace. But anxiety doesn't work that way. The more we try to manage it in our own strength, the heavier it becomes. It drains us emotionally, physically, and spiritually. It distracts us from the present moment, keeping our minds entangled in what-ifs and worst-case scenarios.

But God never intended for us to live this way.

In 1 Peter 5:7, we are given a simple yet profound instruction: *"Cast all your anxiety on Him because He cares for you."* These words are more than just an encouragement; they are a call to action. The word "cast" is not passive—it requires movement, an intentional act of releasing what we are holding onto. To cast our cares on God means to actively place them in His hands, to trust Him with what weighs us down, and to surrender control over the things we cannot change.

But why do we struggle to do this?

At the heart of anxiety is often a lack of trust. When we hold onto our worries, when we replay our fears over and over in our minds, we are, in some ways, believing that we are the ones responsible for holding everything together. We feel as though we have to figure it all out, that if we don't, everything might fall apart. But God's Word tells us the opposite: We don't have to carry these burdens alone.

Peter reminds us *why* we can let go—*because He cares for us.* Not because He is indifferent, not because He is distant, but because He is a loving Father who sees us, knows us, and desires to carry our burdens for us. He is not asking us to cast our cares on Him because He simply can handle them (though He certainly can). He is asking us to do so because He *wants* to. Because He *cares* deeply for us.

Think about that for a moment. The God who created the heavens and the earth, the One who spoke light into existence, who holds the stars in His hands—*He cares about you.* Not just in a general, distant way, but personally, intimately, in every detail of your life. He sees the burdens you carry, the fears that keep you up at night, the struggles you don't always voice out loud. And He is inviting you to release them to Him.

But how do we do that in a practical way? How do we take this command and apply it to the daily struggles we face?

Surrender begins with honesty. God already knows what is weighing on you, but He desires for you to bring it to Him. He wants you to come to Him, to lay it down in prayer, to say, *"Lord, this is what is on my heart. This is what I am carrying. I don't know what to do with it, but I trust You."* It doesn't have to be complicated. It doesn't have to be eloquent. God is not looking for perfect words; He is looking for an open heart.

There is something powerful about speaking our anxieties out loud to God. When we name them, when we acknowledge them, we strip them of their power. Worry thrives in silence, but when we bring it into the light, when we place it in the hands of the One who is greater than our fears, it begins to lose its grip.

But surrender is not just about speaking—it is also about releasing. Many of us pray about our worries, but as soon as we say "Amen," we pick them back up again, carrying them just as we did before. True surrender means choosing to leave them with God. It means reminding ourselves, moment by moment, that He is in control and that we can trust Him with the outcome.

It also means shifting our focus. Anxiety keeps our eyes fixed on our problems, but faith lifts our eyes to God. When we choose to dwell on His promises rather than our fears, when we remind ourselves of His faithfulness, our perspective begins to change. The same problems may still exist, but we see them through the lens of God's power rather than through the lens of our own limitations.

The truth is, life will always bring reasons to worry. There will always be things beyond our control, unknowns that threaten to unsettle us. But God's invitation remains the same: *Cast your cares on Me.* It is not a one-time act, but a daily practice—a continual surrender of our fears, a moment-by-moment choice to trust that He is good, that He is in control, and that He will carry what we were never meant to bear.

There is peace in surrender. When we finally let go, when we release our grip on the things that have held us captive, we find the freedom that God intended for us. We begin to live with a lighter heart, not because the circumstances have necessarily changed, but because we know who holds them.

So, what are you carrying today? What anxieties have been weighing on your heart? God is waiting, His hands open, ready to take them from you. He is not asking you to figure it all out. He is simply asking you to trust Him enough to let go.

**Prayer**

Father, I come before You today with an open heart, ready to surrender the burdens I have been carrying. You see my worries, my anxieties, the thoughts that keep me restless. I confess that too often, I try to handle things on my own, forgetting that You have invited me to place them in Your hands.

Help me, Lord, to truly cast my cares on You. To trust You with what I cannot control. To rest in the truth that You care deeply for me, that You are working in ways I cannot see, that I am not alone in my struggles. Teach me to release my worries to You, not just in word, but in action—to choose faith over fear, surrender over striving.

Fill my heart with Your peace, the peace that surpasses all understanding. Remind me daily that You are my refuge, my strength, and my ever-present help. Thank You for being a God who cares so deeply for me, who carries my burdens when they feel too heavy. I choose to trust You today and every day. In Jesus' name, Amen.

## Faith-Building Action Step

Take a moment today to identify one specific worry or anxiety you have been holding onto. Write it down on a piece of paper, then physically place it in a box, a jar, or even tear it up as a symbolic act of casting it onto God. Each time that worry tries to resurface, remind yourself of 1 Peter 5:7—*"Cast all your anxiety on Him because He cares for you."* Speak it aloud, declare it over your life, and choose to trust that He is in control.

# 12

# Be Still & Know – (Psalm 46:10)

**S**cripture: *"Be still, and know that I am God."* – Psalm 46:10

**Devotional Reflection**

Stillness does not come naturally to us. In a world that constantly demands movement, action, and busyness, the idea of being still feels counterintuitive. We live in a culture that equates productivity with worth, where slowing down is often seen as falling behind. Our schedules are packed, our minds are cluttered, and our hearts are restless. The weight of responsibilities, expectations, and worries keeps us running from one thing to the next, leaving little room to simply pause.

Yet, in the midst of life's chaos, God speaks a simple but powerful command: *"Be still, and know that I am God."* These words are not just a gentle encouragement; they are an invitation into a deeper trust, a call to surrender, a reminder that God is in control even when everything around us feels uncertain.

Being still is not just about physical quietness; it is about an inner posture of trust. It is about ceasing our striving, laying down our anxieties, and resting in the assurance that God is who He says He is. The Hebrew word for "be still" in this verse is *raphah*, which means to let go, to release, to surrender. It is not a passive stillness but an active choice to stop holding onto what was never ours to carry in the first place.

But surrender is hard. Fear tells us that if we stop trying to control things, everything will fall apart. Anxiety convinces us that if we are not constantly working, planning, or fixing, something will go wrong. Our human nature craves control, and the idea of letting go feels risky. What if God doesn't come through? What if things don't turn out the way we hope?

Yet, the second part of this verse gives us the answer: *"Know that I am God."* We are not called to be still just for the sake of stillness; we are called to be still so that we may know Him. To know His nature. To trust His faithfulness. To remember that He is sovereign, that He is present, that He is working even when we cannot see.

When we let go, we are not surrendering to uncertainty—we are surrendering to a God who is unshakable. We are not placing our trust in the unknown; we are placing it in the One who holds all things in His hands. Being still is not about doing nothing; it is about choosing faith over fear, resting in the presence of the One who is greater than our circumstances.

Think about a child in the arms of a loving parent. When that child is afraid, they may cling tightly, resisting comfort, their small hands gripping in desperation. But the moment they allow themselves to relax, to rest, to trust, they find peace. Their parent was holding them all along, but it is only when they stop fighting that they experience the fullness of that embrace.

How often do we cling tightly to our worries, our plans, our fears, believing that our grip is what holds everything together? How often do we resist the very peace God is offering us, convinced that if we let go, we will lose control? But the truth is, we were never meant to carry it all. We were never meant to figure everything out on our own. God is holding us, and He has been all along.

Stillness is an act of trust. It is a declaration that we believe God is in control. It is choosing to stop striving, to stop grasping, to stop running ourselves into exhaustion trying to manage what was never ours to manage. It is choosing to sit at the feet of Jesus, as Mary did, rather than busying ourselves with endless tasks like Martha (Luke 10:38-42).

When we allow ourselves to be still, we create space for God to move. When we quiet the noise of the world, we can hear His voice more clearly. When we release our grip on control, we experience the peace that comes from knowing He is God.

But practically speaking, how do we do this? How do we cultivate stillness in a world that constantly pulls us in a hundred different directions?

It starts with intentionality. Just as we set aside time for work, for relationships, for responsibilities, we must set aside time to be still before God. This does not mean that life stops, but it means that we carve out moments to pause, to breathe, to remind ourselves of who He is.

It means creating rhythms of rest, whether through prayer, meditating on His Word, or simply sitting in His presence without an agenda. It means choosing to trust even when we don't have all the answers, reminding ourselves that God is not asking us to figure everything out—He is asking us to trust Him.

Being still is not about escaping reality; it is about anchoring ourselves in the only reality that truly matters: God is in control. He is our refuge, our strength, our ever-present help in trouble (Psalm 46:1). The storms may rage, the uncertainties may press in, but He remains unshaken.

So, what is keeping you from stillness today? What fears, what anxieties, what burdens are you carrying that God is asking you to release? He is not calling you to figure it all out—He is calling you to rest in the truth that He already has.

He is God. He is faithful. And He is inviting you to be still and know.

**Prayer**

Father, I come before You today, weary from striving, burdened by the weight of things I cannot control. You see the anxieties that fill my heart, the thoughts that race through my mind. I confess that too often, I try to manage things on my own, forgetting that You have invited me to rest in You.

Help me to be still, to release my need for control, to surrender my fears into Your hands. Teach me to trust that You are working, even when I cannot see. Remind me that You are God, that You are faithful, that You are always present. When I am tempted to let anxiety take over, draw me back to Your peace.

Fill my heart with the assurance that You are in control. Help me to rest in Your presence, to trust in Your timing, to walk in faith rather than fear. Thank You for being my refuge, my strength, my unshakable foundation. I choose today to be still and know that You are God. In Jesus' name, Amen.

## Faith-Building Action Step

Set aside ten minutes today to be still before God. Find a quiet place, close your eyes, and take a deep breath. Release your worries into His hands. As you do, meditate on Psalm 46:10, letting its truth settle in your heart. Whenever anxiety rises, return to this moment of stillness, reminding yourself that God is in control.

# 13

# God's Perfect Peace – (Isaiah 26:3)

**S**cripture: *"You will keep in perfect peace those whose minds are steadfast, because they trust in you."* – Isaiah 26:3

**Devotional Reflection**

Peace. It is something we all long for, yet so often find elusive. The world tells us that peace comes when circumstances are favorable—when our finances are secure, when our relationships are thriving, when our health is strong, when life is free of difficulties. But as soon as something shifts, as soon as uncertainty enters the picture, that sense of peace crumbles, revealing just how fragile it truly was.

But God offers something different. He promises not just fleeting moments of peace, but *perfect peace*. A peace that is unshaken by circumstances. A peace that is not dependent on external stability, but rather on something far deeper—on trust in Him.

Isaiah 26:3 speaks directly to this truth: *"You will keep in perfect peace those whose minds are steadfast, because they trust in you."* These words were not spoken in a time of ease; they were written in the midst of trials, spoken as a declaration of confidence in God's faithfulness despite the challenges surrounding His people. This peace is not the absence of trouble but the presence of an unwavering trust in God in the midst of it.

Yet, how often do we seek peace in everything *but* God?

We search for it in control, trying to manage every outcome, believing that if we just plan enough, work enough, prepare enough, we can secure our own peace. But control is an illusion, and the moment something slips beyond our grasp, anxiety creeps in.

We search for it in people, in relationships, in approval, hoping that if we are loved enough, valued enough, accepted enough, we will finally feel at rest. But human relationships, no matter how strong, are not meant to bear the weight of our deepest need for security. When people fail us or circumstances change, the peace we once felt disappears.

We search for it in temporary distractions—numbing ourselves with entertainment, busyness, or anything that keeps us from facing what is stirring in our hearts. But distractions do not heal; they only delay. And once the noise fades, the unrest remains.

The peace that God offers is different. It is a peace that

surpasses all understanding (Philippians 4:7). It does not make sense in the natural. It is the kind of peace that allows us to stand firm when life is uncertain, to remain steady when storms arise, to breathe deeply even when the future is unknown.

But how do we step into this perfect peace?

Isaiah gives us the answer: *"Those whose minds are steadfast, because they trust in You."* Perfect peace is not something we achieve—it is something we receive as we fix our minds on God, as we choose to trust Him with every part of our lives.

To have a steadfast mind means to be anchored in truth, to set our focus not on what we *see*, but on who God *is*. It means that when fear rises, we return to His promises. When anxiety whispers lies, we declare His truth. When worry tempts us to take control, we surrender again, knowing that He is faithful.

Trust is the foundation of this peace. Trust is what allows us to rest when life is uncertain, to remain unshaken even when we don't understand. Trust is what enables us to place our anxieties in God's hands, believing that He is good, that He is sovereign, that He is working even when we cannot see.

But trust is not always easy. There are moments when doubts creep in, when circumstances feel overwhelming, when peace feels distant. In those moments, we must make the choice to refocus—to turn our eyes back to Him, to remind ourselves of His faithfulness, to stand on His Word rather than on our emotions.

Think of Peter walking on the water toward Jesus (Matthew 14:28-31). As long as his eyes were fixed on Jesus, he did the impossible—he walked on the waves, steady in the midst of the storm. But the moment he looked at the wind and the waves, fear took over, and he began to sink. The storm had not changed; what changed was his focus.

How often do we do the same? As long as we keep our eyes on God, we experience His peace, His presence, His strength. But the moment we shift our focus to the storm, to the uncertainties, to the "what ifs," peace is replaced with fear. The waves seem bigger. The wind seems stronger. And we begin to sink under the weight of it all.

But even then, Jesus reaches out His hand, just as He did with Peter. Even when we lose focus, even when we falter, His grace remains. He lifts us up. He reminds us that we were never meant to walk this journey alone.

True peace is not found in the absence of trouble, but in the presence of God. It is found in knowing that no matter what happens, we are held by the One who never fails. It is found in resting in the truth that He is in control, even when life feels uncertain. It is found in surrender, in trust, in fixing our minds on Him rather than on our fears.

This perfect peace is available to you today. It is not reserved for the strong or the unshakable. It is for the weary, the anxious, the ones who feel like they are sinking. It is for those who choose to trust, even when trust feels hard.

So what are you focusing on today? Where is your mind fixed? Are your thoughts consumed by worry, by fear, by all the unknowns? Or are you choosing to fix your mind on the One who holds all things together?

His peace is waiting. Not just any peace, but *perfect peace*. A peace that does not waver, that does not depend on circumstances, that is rooted in the unwavering truth of who He is.

And all He asks is that you trust Him.

**Prayer**

Father, I come before You today, longing for the peace that only You can give. My heart is often restless, my mind filled with worries, my soul weighed down by uncertainty. But Your Word promises that You will keep in perfect peace those whose minds are steadfast, those who trust in You.

Teach me, Lord, to fix my mind on You. When fear rises, help me to return to Your truth. When anxiety threatens to overwhelm me, remind me that You are in control. Strengthen my trust in You, even when I don't understand, even when the path ahead is unclear.

Fill my heart with Your peace, a peace that surpasses understanding. Let it steady me in the storms, anchor me in the uncertainties, remind me that I am held by a God who never fails. Thank You that Your peace is not dependent on my circumstances, but on Your unchanging faithfulness. I choose today to trust You completely. In Jesus' name, Amen.

**Faith-Building Action Step**

Throughout the day, when anxiety or fear arises, pause and shift your focus. Speak Isaiah 26:3 aloud, declaring its truth over your life. Take a deep breath, refocus your mind on God, and remind yourself: *He will keep me in perfect peace as I trust in Him.*

# 14

# Walking in Boldness – (2 Timothy 1:7)

**S**cripture: *"For God has not given us a spirit of fear, but of power and of love and of a sound mind."* – 2 Timothy 1:7

**Devotional Reflection**

Fear has a way of making itself at home in our hearts. It creeps in quietly, whispering lies that hold us back, convincing us that we are not enough, that we are not capable, that we are too weak to move forward. It tells us to shrink back when we should step forward, to remain silent when we should speak, to stay where it's comfortable rather than walk in faith. Fear thrives in hesitation, in uncertainty, in the moments when we doubt who we are and what God has called us to do.

But fear was never meant to have power over us.

Paul's words to Timothy in **2 Timothy 1:7** are a direct challenge to the spirit of fear that so often tries to control our lives: *"For God has not given us a spirit of fear, but of power* *and of love and of a sound mind."* This verse is more than encouragement—it is a declaration of truth. Fear is not from God. It is not His desire for us to live in timidity, to be held back by anxiety, to allow doubt to dictate our decisions. Instead, He has given us something far greater—power, love, and a sound mind.

But what does it mean to walk in boldness? What does it look like to live free from fear when it so often feels like fear is woven into the fabric of our daily lives?

Walking in boldness does not mean we will never feel afraid. It does not mean we will never face moments of uncertainty or hesitation. Boldness is not the absence of fear; it is the choice to move forward despite it. It is the choice to trust that what God has placed within us is greater than the fears that try to hold us back.

When Paul wrote these words to Timothy, he was speaking to a young leader who likely struggled with insecurity, with timidity, with the weight of responsibility. Timothy was stepping into a calling that required courage, a life of ministry that would not always be easy. And yet, Paul did not tell him to muster up strength on his own. He did not tell him to be bold in his own ability. Instead, he reminded him of what God had already given him—*a spirit of power, of love, and of a sound mind.*

This is the foundation of boldness.

**Power.** The strength to do what God has called us to do, even when we feel weak. This is not a power that comes from our own abilities, but from the Holy Spirit within us. It is the same power that raised Christ from the dead (Romans 8:11), the same power that enables us to stand firm, to step forward in faith, to do what seems impossible. When we feel inadequate, God's power reminds us that we are not doing this alone.

**Love.** Fear often tries to isolate us, to make us focus inward on our own insecurities and doubts. But love shifts our perspective. Love is outward-focused, drawing us closer to God and to others. When we walk in love, we are no longer controlled by fear of rejection, by fear of failure, by fear of not being enough. Love casts out fear (1 John 4:18), replacing it with confidence that we are fully known and fully loved by God.

**A Sound Mind.** Fear thrives in confusion, in chaos, in the uncertainty of what might happen. But God has given us a sound mind—a mind that is steady, secure, anchored in truth. This means we do not have to be controlled by anxious thoughts, by what-ifs, by the lies of the enemy. We have the ability to think clearly, to discern truth, to stand firm in the promises of God.

So how do we walk in boldness when fear still tries to take hold?

It begins with knowing who we are in Christ. Fear loses its grip when we understand that our identity is not in our weaknesses, not in our failures, not in the opinions of others, but in the unshakable truth that we are children of God. We are chosen, we are called, we are empowered by the Spirit of God Himself.

Walking in boldness also requires stepping out in faith, even when we don't feel ready. Fear often waits for us at the edge of obedience, trying to convince us to stay where it's safe, where it's familiar. But boldness is stepping forward anyway, knowing that God is already ahead of us. It is trusting that He equips those He calls, that He strengthens us as we walk, that He is working even in our weaknesses.

Think of Moses, standing before the burning bush, arguing with God about why he wasn't qualified to lead (Exodus 3-4). Think of Gideon, hiding in fear, doubting that he could be the one to deliver Israel (Judges 6). Think of Peter, stepping out of the boat onto the water, only to falter when he looked at the waves (Matthew 14:29-30). Time and time again, God has chosen people who felt unqualified, who struggled with fear, who doubted their own abilities. And time and time again, He has shown that boldness is not about being fearless—it is about trusting Him enough to take the next step.

So what is fear holding you back from today? What has God placed on your heart that you have been too afraid to step into? The fear may feel real, but it is not your identity. God has not given you a spirit of fear. He has given you power. He has given you love. He has given you a sound mind.

The next time fear tries to hold you back, remind yourself of this truth. Declare it over your life. Step forward in faith, knowing that you are not alone. The God who calls you is the God who equips you. The God who leads you is the God who strengthens you. And the God who has placed boldness within you is the God who will see you through.

## Prayer

Father, I come before You today, acknowledging the fears that try to hold me back. You see the moments when I hesitate, when I doubt, when I let fear have more power than it should. But Your Word reminds me that You have not given me a spirit of fear, but of power, love, and a sound mind.

Help me to walk in the boldness You have given me. Strengthen me when I feel weak. Remind me that my confidence is not in myself, but in You. When fear tries to creep in, help me to stand firm in Your truth. When doubts arise, let me rest in the knowledge that You are with me, guiding me, equipping me, empowering me.

I surrender my fears to You today. I choose to trust You, to step forward in faith, to walk in the boldness that comes from knowing I am Yours. Thank You for being my strength, my refuge, my ever-present help. In Jesus' name, Amen.

## Faith-Building Action Step

Identify one area in your life where fear has been holding you back. Take a step today—no matter how small—to move forward in faith. Speak 2 Timothy 1:7 over yourself, declaring that fear has no place in your life. Trust that God has given you everything you need to walk boldly in Him.

# 15

# The Power of Surrender – (Proverbs 3:5-6)

**S**cripture: *"Trust in the Lord with all your heart and lean not on your own understanding; in all your ways submit to him, and he will make your paths straight."* – Proverbs 3:5-6

**Devotional Reflection**

Surrender is not something that comes naturally to us. From the time we are young, we are taught to take control, to be independent, to figure things out for ourselves. The world applauds self-sufficiency, rewarding those who seem to have everything under control. But what happens when control slips through our fingers? What do we do when no amount of planning, effort, or worry can fix what is broken, change what is unchangeable, or guarantee the outcome we desperately want?

Anxiety thrives in the tension between what we can control

and what we cannot. It feeds on uncertainty, whispering that if we just try a little harder, hold on a little tighter, or think through every possible scenario, we can somehow secure peace. But Proverbs 3:5-6 offers us a different way—*a way of trust, a way of surrender, a way of releasing our need to figure everything out and placing our confidence in the One who already knows the way forward.*

*"Trust in the Lord with all your heart and lean not on your own understanding."*

Trust requires letting go. It means releasing our grip on the things we cannot control and placing them in God's hands. It is not a half-hearted belief, not a backup plan in case our own efforts fail, but a full and complete reliance on God. *With all your heart.* Not just with our words, not just on Sundays, not just when life is going well, but in every moment, in every situation, in every unknown.

And yet, trusting God fully can feel difficult. Our understanding of life, of circumstances, of outcomes is limited. We see only a small piece of the picture, and when things do not go as we expect, it is easy to question whether God is truly in control. We want to lean on what makes sense to us, to trust in what we can see, to rely on our own reasoning. But Scripture warns against this—*lean not on your own understanding.*

Our understanding is shaped by our emotions, by past experiences, by fears, by the immediate realities in front of us. God's understanding, on the other hand, is eternal. He sees the beginning and the end. He knows the purpose behind the waiting, the growth that happens in the uncertainty, the deeper work He is doing in us even when things don't make sense.

Surrender is not a sign of weakness; it is a sign of trust. It is the act of laying down our worries, our plans, our need for control and saying, *"God, I trust You more than I trust myself. I trust that Your ways are higher than my ways, that Your wisdom is greater than my own, that You are working all things for good even when I do not understand."*

*"In all your ways submit to Him, and He will make your paths straight."*

Submission is a difficult word in today's culture. It carries connotations of giving up, of being powerless, of losing autonomy. But biblical surrender is something different. It is not about losing ourselves; it is about finding ourselves in God's perfect will. It is not about passivity; it is about actively choosing to let God lead.

To submit to God in all our ways means that we seek Him first. It means we do not rely on our own wisdom but invite Him into every decision, every step, every unknown. It means we stop striving to make things happen in our own strength and instead trust in His timing, His provision, His plan.

And what does He promise in return? *He will make your paths straight.*

This does not mean the path will always be easy, or that every desire we have will be fulfilled exactly as we wish. It means that when we trust Him, when we surrender, when we stop trying to figure everything out on our own, He leads us in the way we are meant to go. He removes obstacles that should not be there, aligns our steps with His will, and directs our journey in ways that we could never orchestrate on our own.

But surrender is not a one-time decision. It is a daily choice. Each morning, we must decide to lay down our worries. Each time anxiety rises, we must choose to place our trust back in God. Each time fear whispers that we are losing control, we must remind ourselves that we were never meant to carry the weight of control in the first place.

Think about Jesus in the Garden of Gethsemane. As He faced the cross, He prayed, *"Father, if You are willing, take this cup from Me; yet not My will, but Yours be done."* (Luke 22:42). In His most human moment, He surrendered completely to the Father's will. He trusted that even in suffering, even in the unknown, God's plan was greater.

Surrender is not about giving up—it is about giving *over.* It is about handing over our fears, our uncertainties, our desperate need for control and placing them in the hands of the One who holds all things together. It is about believing that God's way is better, even when we cannot yet see where the path is leading.

So what is God asking you to surrender today? What have you been holding onto, trying to manage in your own strength, that He is inviting you to release?

Let go. Open your hands. Trust Him fully. His plans are

greater than yours, His wisdom higher than yours, His love deeper than you can imagine. When you surrender, you are not losing—you are gaining the peace that comes from knowing that the One who leads you is faithful.

## Prayer

Father, I come before You today, carrying burdens that I was never meant to bear. You see the things I have been holding onto, the worries I have clung to, the fears that have kept me from fully trusting You. I confess that I have often leaned on my own understanding, trying to control what was never mine to control.

But today, I choose surrender. I choose to trust You with all my heart. I lay down my plans, my fears, my anxieties at Your feet, believing that Your ways are higher, that Your wisdom is greater, that Your love for me is unshakable.

Teach me to walk in surrender daily. When fear rises, remind me of Your faithfulness. When I do not understand, help me to trust that You are leading me. When I am tempted to take control, gently guide me back to the truth that You are in control.

Thank You, Lord, for being my refuge, my strength, my ever-present help. Thank You for the peace that comes with surrender. I trust You, and I give You every part of my life. In Jesus' name, Amen.

## Faith-Building Action Step

Take a moment today to reflect on what you have been holding onto. Write it down—whether it's a specific worry, a situation, or a fear of the unknown. Then, in an act of surrender, physically place it in God's hands. If you need to, kneel in prayer, lift your hands, or even write down Proverbs 3:5-6 as a reminder. Each time that fear tries to creep back in, return to this moment of surrender and choose again to trust that God is leading you.

# 16

# Releasing Worry to God – (Matthew 6:34)

S **cripture:** *"Therefore do not worry about tomorrow, for tomorrow will worry about itself. Each day has enough trouble of its own."* – Matthew 6:34

**Devotional Reflection**

Worry is an unwelcome companion, creeping into our thoughts when we least expect it. It often starts with a small concern, a fleeting question about the future, but before long, it takes root, growing into an overwhelming sense of unease. It fills our minds with endless "what ifs" and worst-case scenarios, keeping us restless, distracted, and drained. Worry convinces us that if we think about something long enough, if we prepare for every possible outcome, we can somehow control what happens next. But no matter how much we worry, the future remains beyond our grasp.

Jesus speaks directly to this struggle in Matthew 6:34, offering a simple yet profound instruction: *"Do not worry about tomorrow, for tomorrow will worry about itself. Each day has enough trouble of its own."* At first glance, this might seem easier said than done. After all, how can we simply stop worrying when the uncertainties of life feel so real, when there are bills to pay, decisions to make, loved ones to care for, and responsibilities that seem endless? But Jesus isn't offering an empty command—He is inviting us into a way of living that frees us from the weight of unnecessary burdens.

When Jesus spoke these words, He had just finished reminding His listeners that God takes care of the birds of the air and the flowers of the field. If God provides for even the smallest details of creation, how much more will He provide for His children? Worry, at its core, is often rooted in a lack of trust. It stems from the fear that maybe God won't come through this time, that maybe He isn't paying attention to our needs, that maybe we are on our own. But Jesus challenges that mindset, calling us to shift our focus away from worry and toward trust in our heavenly Father.

Worry does not change the future; it only steals our peace in the present. It keeps us trapped in a cycle of anxiety, constantly looking ahead to what *might* happen instead of living fully in what God has given us today. Jesus understands this tendency, which is why He gently redirects us: *"Each day has enough trouble of its own."* In other words, we are not meant to carry tomorrow's burdens today. We are called to live one moment at a time, trusting that God will provide the strength, wisdom, and grace we need for *this* day.

Releasing worry to God is not about ignoring reality or pretending that difficulties don't exist. It is about choosing to trust that God is already in our tomorrows. He sees what we cannot see. He knows the details of our future just as clearly as He knows our present. And He has already made a way.

So why do we still hold onto worry?

Sometimes, we believe that worrying gives us a sense of control. We replay situations in our minds, analyzing every possible outcome, thinking that if we just prepare enough, we can avoid disappointment or pain. But control is an illusion. No amount of planning can account for every variable, and no amount of worrying can prevent unexpected challenges. The only true security we have is found in surrender—placing our trust not in our ability to predict the future, but in God's ability to lead us through it.

Other times, we hold onto worry because we don't know what to do with our fears. We let them pile up in our hearts, carrying them as if they are ours to bear alone. But Jesus offers us another way. In **1 Peter 5:7**, we are reminded: *"Cast all your anxiety on Him because He cares for you."* God is not asking us to suppress our worries or pretend they don't exist. He is inviting us to bring them to Him, to release them into His capable hands, to trust that He is already working on our behalf.

But releasing worry is not a one-time decision; it is a daily practice. Each morning, we have a choice: Will we carry our burdens alone, or will we lay them at the feet of Jesus? Each time anxiety rises, we can either dwell on it, letting it spiral into fear, or we can turn to God in prayer, choosing to trust that He is in control.

Think about a child learning to walk. A loving parent doesn't expect them to figure it out all at once. The child stumbles, reaches for support, sometimes falls, but the parent is always there—encouraging, steadying, guiding. Our heavenly Father is the same way. He does not condemn us when we struggle with worry. Instead, He invites us to take His hand, to lean on His strength, to trust that even when the road ahead is unclear, He is walking with us.

Jesus calls us to a life of peace, not a life consumed by worry. This doesn't mean that difficult circumstances won't arise. It doesn't mean that we will always know what comes next. But it does mean that we do not have to face the unknown alone. When we release worry to God, we are making a declaration of faith—we are saying, *"Lord, I trust You more than I trust my fears. I believe that You are for me, that You are leading me, that You will provide exactly what I need at the right time."*

So, what is weighing on your heart today? What future concern is stealing your peace in the present? God is already there. He has already prepared the way. He is asking you to let go—not because He wants to take something from you, but because He wants to *give* you something better: the deep, abiding peace that comes from trusting in Him.

Take a deep breath. Release the weight of tomorrow. And rest in the truth that the God who holds the future is holding *you*.

## Prayer

Father, I come before You today with the worries that have been weighing on my heart. You see the thoughts that keep me up at night, the concerns that threaten to steal my peace. I confess that I have often tried to carry these burdens on my own, forgetting that You have invited me to release them into Your hands.

Help me, Lord, to trust You more. Teach me to let go of the things I cannot control and to rest in the truth that You are already working in my future. When worry rises, remind me of Your faithfulness. When fear tries to take hold, fill me with Your peace.

I surrender my anxieties to You today. I choose to live fully in the present, trusting that You will provide for tomorrow just as You have always provided before. Thank You for being my refuge, my strength, my constant help in every situation. I place my trust in You, knowing that You are in control. In Jesus' name, Amen.

## Faith-Building Action Step

Take a piece of paper and write down the worries that have been on your heart. One by one, pray over each one, releasing them to God. Then, physically destroy the paper—rip it up, throw it away, or place it in a box as a symbol of surrender. Let this be a reminder that those worries no longer belong to you; they are in God's hands. Whenever anxiety tries to return, recall this moment and choose again to trust Him.

# 17

# Finding Strength in Weakness – (2 Corinthians 12:9)

**Scripture:** *"But he said to me, 'My grace is sufficient for you, for my power is made perfect in weakness.' Therefore, I will boast all the more gladly about my weaknesses, so that Christ's power may rest on me."* – 2 Corinthians 12:9

## Devotional Reflection

Weakness is not something we like to admit. We live in a world that celebrates strength, resilience, and self-sufficiency. From a young age, we are taught to push through, to be strong, to never let anyone see us struggle. We convince ourselves that if we try hard enough, if we work long enough, if we put on a brave face, we can handle anything that comes our way. But what happens when we reach the end of our own strength? What do we do when the weight of life becomes too much to carry, when exhaustion sets in, when our best efforts still aren't enough?

Paul knew what it felt like to be weak. In **2 Corinthians 12**, he speaks of a thorn in his flesh, something that caused him deep struggle—something he begged God to remove. We don't know exactly what this thorn was, but we do know that it was a source of pain, something that made Paul feel inadequate, something that reminded him of his own limitations. He pleaded with God, not once, not twice, but three times to take it away. And yet, God's response was not to remove the struggle, but to reveal a deeper truth: *"My grace is sufficient for you, for my power is made perfect in weakness."*

This is not the answer we often want to hear. When we are struggling, when we feel weak, when we are overwhelmed by anxiety or fear, we want God to take it away immediately. We want Him to fix the problem, to make us strong, to remove whatever is making life difficult. But instead, God invites us into something greater—*to experience His strength in the midst of our weakness.*

Weakness is not something to be ashamed of. It is not a sign of failure or lack of faith. It is an invitation to rely on God in ways we never would if we only relied on ourselves. When we are strong in our own ability, it is easy to forget our need for Him. But when we come to the end of ourselves, when we have no choice but to lean on His grace, that is where His power is most clearly seen.

Think about a child learning to walk. At first, their steps are shaky, unsteady. They reach for something to hold onto, needing the steady hand of a parent to guide them. The parent does not shame the child for their weakness. Instead, they offer support, knowing that in time, the child will grow stronger. But even in those early, wobbly steps, the parent's presence is enough. The child is not walking alone.

God is the same way with us. He does not look at our weakness with disappointment. He does not expect us to have it all together, to figure everything out on our own. He simply asks us to trust that *His* strength is enough. That His grace will carry us when we feel like we cannot take another step. That His power will sustain us, even when we feel like we are falling apart.

We often think of strength as the ability to stand tall, to be unshaken, to press forward without struggle. But God's definition of strength looks different. His strength is found in surrender. His strength is found in the quiet trust of a heart that knows it does not have to have all the answers. His strength is found in the one who admits, *"Lord, I can't do this on my own."*

And that is where grace steps in.

Grace is not just God's forgiveness; it is His empowerment. It is His presence working in us, sustaining us, filling the gaps where we fall short. It is the reminder that we do not have to be enough, because *He* is enough. His grace does not remove our weaknesses, but it transforms them. It turns them into a testimony of His power, a story of how He carried us when we could not carry ourselves.

Paul's response to God's answer is remarkable: *"Therefore, I will boast all the more gladly about my weaknesses, so that Christ's power may rest on me."* Boasting in weakness is the opposite of what the world tells us to do. But Paul had come to understand a deep truth—his weakness was not something to be hidden or avoided. It was the very place where God's power was most evident.

What if we began to see our own struggles that way? What if, instead of feeling ashamed of our weaknesses, we saw them as an opportunity to experience more of God's grace? What if we stopped striving to be strong on our own and instead learned to rest in *His* strength?

Jesus Himself modeled this for us. In the Garden of Gethsemane, as He faced the cross, He was overwhelmed to the point of sweating drops of blood. In that moment, He did not rely on His own strength—He cried out to the Father. He surrendered, trusting that God's plan was greater than the pain He was about to endure. And because of His willingness to walk through weakness, through suffering, through surrender, we now have victory.

The same is true in our lives. Our weaknesses are not the end of the story. The struggles we face, the battles we fight, the moments when we feel like we cannot go on—these are the places where God's power is most evident. When we surrender our weaknesses to Him, when we stop trying to carry everything on our own, when we allow His grace to be enough, we find a strength that is not our own.

So, what weakness have you been hiding? What burden have you been carrying, believing that you have to be strong enough to handle it alone? God is inviting you to lay it down. To stop striving. To rest in the assurance that *His* strength is enough for you.

You do not have to have it all together. You do not have to be strong in yourself. You simply have to trust that the One who holds you will not let you fall.

His grace is sufficient. His power is made perfect in your weakness. And He is with you, carrying you, every step of the way.

## Prayer

Father, I come before You today, feeling the weight of my own weakness. There are moments when I feel inadequate, when I struggle, when I reach the end of my own strength. But Your Word reminds me that Your grace is sufficient, that Your power is made perfect in my weakness.

Help me to stop striving in my own strength. Teach me to rely fully on You. When I feel overwhelmed, remind me that I do not have to carry this alone. When I feel weak, fill me with Your power. Let my struggles become a testimony of Your faithfulness, a story of how You carried me when I could not carry myself.

I surrender my weaknesses to You. I lay down my burdens, my fears, my inadequacies, knowing that You are enough. Thank You for Your grace, for Your strength, for the constant reminder that I am never alone. I trust You, Lord, with every part of my life. In Jesus' name, Amen.

**Faith-Building Action Step**

Take a moment to reflect on an area of your life where you feel weak, overwhelmed, or inadequate. Instead of trying to push through in your own strength, bring it before God in prayer. Speak 2 Corinthians 12:9 over yourself, declaring that His grace is sufficient for you. Each time you feel the temptation to rely on your own strength, pause, surrender, and remind yourself that *His power is made perfect in your weakness.*

# 18

# Week 3: Strengthening Your Faith

F aith is like a muscle—it grows stronger through testing, perseverance, and trust. When trials come, they are not meant to break you, but to refine you. This week, we will discover how to stand firm in faith, endure through challenges, and deepen our confidence in God's unshakable promises.

# 19

# The Refining Fire of Trials – (James 1:2-4)

S **cripture:** *"Consider it pure joy, my brothers and sisters, whenever you face trials of many kinds, because you know that the testing of your faith produces perseverance. Let perseverance finish its work so that you may be mature and complete, not lacking anything."* – James 1:2-4

### Devotional Reflection

Trials are an inevitable part of life. They arrive uninvited, disrupting our plans, shaking our confidence, and testing the very foundation of our faith. They come in many forms— disappointments, losses, setbacks, struggles we never anticipated. In these moments, it is natural to ask, *Why is this happening? Where is God in all of this?* When we are in the midst of suffering, joy is often the last thing on our minds. And yet, James offers a radically different perspective: *Consider it pure joy whenever you face trials.*

Joy? In trials? The idea seems almost impossible. When hardships press in on us, when our hearts are weary and our prayers feel unanswered, how can we possibly embrace joy? The world tells us that joy is found in ease, in comfort, in a life free from difficulties. But the Bible presents a different truth—one that challenges our human instincts. Joy is not the absence of trials; it is the deep confidence that God is using those very trials to shape us, strengthen us, and refine our faith.

James does not say *if* you face trials, but *when.* Trials are not a possibility; they are a certainty. Faith is not proven in the absence of hardship but in the endurance of it. It is in the refining fire of trials that we learn to trust God at a deeper level, to let go of self-reliance, and to discover a faith that is unshakable.

Imagine a piece of gold in the hands of a skilled refiner. In its raw state, it is valuable but impure. It contains imperfections—traces of other elements that diminish its worth. The only way to purify gold is to subject it to intense heat. The fire burns away impurities, leaving behind something stronger, purer, more beautiful. The process is painful, but the result is transformation. This is the image James gives us of our faith. God, the Master Refiner, allows us to walk through the fire not to destroy us, but to refine us.

Trials reveal what is in our hearts. When life is easy, it is simple to declare trust in God. But when storms arise—when prayers seem unanswered, when losses feel unbearable—our faith is tested. Do we truly believe that God is good, even when circumstances are not? Do we trust His timing, even when waiting is painful? Do we hold onto His promises, even when we cannot yet see their fulfillment?

James tells us that *the testing of your faith produces perseverance.* Trials are not pointless. They are not random acts of suffering. They serve a purpose—to strengthen our endurance. Without resistance, faith remains weak. But through challenges, our spiritual muscles grow. Each time we choose to trust God in hardship, our faith is stretched and strengthened. It is in the waiting, the enduring, the pressing on that we develop perseverance—a faith that is not easily shaken, a faith that remains steadfast regardless of what life brings.

But perseverance is not the final goal. James continues, *Let perseverance finish its work so that you may be mature and complete, not lacking anything.* God's desire is not simply for us to endure trials, but to be transformed by them. The refining fire does not leave us the same; it produces maturity. It deepens our faith, shapes our character, and aligns our hearts more fully with His. There are lessons we can only learn in the fire. There is a depth of trust that only develops in seasons of uncertainty. There is a closeness to God that we experience most profoundly in the moments when we have nowhere else to turn.

Think about the great men and women of faith in Scripture. Joseph, betrayed by his brothers and sold into slavery, endured years of hardship before seeing God's plan unfold. Yet, through the trial, God was preparing him to save a nation. Job, after losing everything, declared, *"But He knows the way that I take; when He has tested me, I will come forth as gold"* (Job 23:10). Paul, who faced imprisonment, beatings, and shipwrecks, could still say, *"I consider that our present sufferings are not worth comparing with the glory that will be revealed in us"* (Romans 8:18). Their trials were not wasted. Their faith was refined, their character was strengthened, and their trust in God became unwavering.

Maybe today, you find yourself in the fire. Perhaps you are walking through a season of uncertainty, facing a trial that feels too heavy to bear. The road ahead may be unclear, the answers you seek may not have come, and the weight of your circumstances may feel overwhelming. But hear this truth: You are not being destroyed—you are being refined. The trial you are facing is not meant to break you but to strengthen you. God is not absent in your suffering; He is present in the midst of it, working in ways you cannot yet see.

James does not tell us to be joyful *for* the trial, but *in* the trial. There is a difference. We do not celebrate suffering itself, but we rejoice in what God is producing through it. We trust that He is using this season to deepen our faith, to shape our hearts, and to prepare us for what lies ahead. The fire is not comfortable, but it is necessary. And when we emerge from it, we will be stronger, purer, more deeply rooted in Him.

Hold onto this promise: *"And after you have suffered a little while, the God of all grace, who has called you to His eternal glory in Christ, will Himself restore, confirm, strengthen, and establish you"* (1 Peter 5:10). The suffering is temporary, but the work God is doing in you is eternal. He is refining you, not to leave you broken, but to make you whole.

Whatever trial you are facing today, lift your eyes. God is

with you in the fire. Trust in the work He is doing, even if you cannot yet see the finished result. He is shaping you into something beautiful, something unshakable, something that reflects His glory. And one day, you will look back and see that every trial, every tear, every moment of refining was leading you to something greater.

You are not alone. You are not forgotten. You are being refined in the fire of His love. And when perseverance has finished its work, you will emerge, not broken, but complete—lacking nothing.

## Prayer

Father, I come before You in the midst of trials, knowing that You are at work even when I cannot see it. When the fire feels too hot, when the road feels too long, remind me that You are refining me, strengthening me, and drawing me closer to You. Help me to trust You in the process, to embrace the work You are doing in my heart, and to find joy in knowing that You are making me more like You. Give me perseverance to endure, faith to believe, and peace to rest in Your promises. Thank You for Your love, for Your presence, and for the assurance that I am never alone. In Jesus' name, Amen.

## Faith-Building Action Step

Take a moment to reflect on a trial you have faced or are currently walking through. Write down how God might be using it to strengthen your faith, to refine your character, or to draw you closer to Him. If you are struggling to see the purpose, ask Him to reveal His work in your life. Keep this as a reminder that trials are not wasted—they are the refining fire through which He is making you whole.

# 20

# God's Grace is Enough – (Romans 8:28)

**S**cripture: *"And we know that in all things God works for the good of those who love Him, who have been called according to His purpose." –* Romans 8:28

### Devotional Reflection

There are moments in life when everything seems to fall apart. Circumstances shift unexpectedly, dreams unravel, and the plans we once held tightly slip through our fingers. In these moments, it can be hard to believe that anything good can come from our pain, that there could be purpose in our suffering. When trials weigh heavily on our hearts, we long for answers, for clarity, for a glimpse of the reason behind our struggles. And yet, more often than not, we are met with silence.

It is in these moments that Romans 8:28 stands as a beacon of hope. Paul, writing to the believers in Rome, declares a truth that has sustained countless souls through hardship: *"And we know that in all things God works for the good of those who love Him, who have been called according to His purpose."* These words are not a shallow reassurance; they are a profound declaration of God's sovereignty, His goodness, and the sufficiency of His grace.

But let's be honest—when we are in the midst of hardship, it does not always feel like things are working out for good. There are seasons when prayers go unanswered, when suffering lingers, when the weight of grief and disappointment presses down relentlessly. In those times, we wrestle with doubt, wondering, *Is God really working in this? Can anything good truly come from this pain?*

Paul's words remind us of something crucial: *we know.* Not *we hope,* not *we think,* but *we know* that God is at work in all things. This is not a blind optimism that ignores reality, nor is it a vague assurance that everything will eventually feel good. It is a confidence rooted in the character of God Himself. He is a Redeemer, a Restorer, a God who does not waste a single moment of our lives. Even in suffering, even in loss, even in seasons of waiting and uncertainty, He is working for our good.

But what does *good* mean? It is easy to interpret this verse through the lens of human desires, assuming that God's promise means He will always make things turn out the way we want. That the pain will be removed, the difficulty resolved, the broken pieces put back together exactly as we envision. But God's definition of *good* is far deeper than our own. His goal is not just our comfort, but our transformation. His priority is not our temporary ease, but our eternal wholeness.

Consider a skilled artist working on a masterpiece. From the outside, the process may look messy. There are brushstrokes that seem misplaced, colors that appear out of sync, details that do not yet make sense. If we were to pause and judge the painting midway, it might look like chaos. But the artist sees the full picture. Every stroke, every shade, every detail serves a purpose, contributing to the beauty of the final piece.

This is how God works in our lives. The moments that feel disjointed, the seasons that seem senseless, the trials that break us—He is weaving them all together into something beyond what we can imagine. The promise of Romans 8:28 is not that every individual moment will feel good, but that in the hands of a sovereign and loving God, nothing is wasted.

We see this truth echoed throughout Scripture. Joseph, betrayed by his brothers, sold into slavery, and wrongfully imprisoned, must have wondered where God was in the midst of his suffering. Yet, years later, as he stood in a position of authority, saving the very brothers who had wronged him, he declared, *"You intended to harm me, but God intended it for good to accomplish what is now being done, the saving of many lives"* (Genesis 50:20). What seemed like senseless suffering was, in fact, part of God's greater plan.

The same is true for us. The pain we endure, the trials we face, the prayers that seem unanswered—none of it is meaningless. God is at work in ways we cannot yet see, crafting a story of redemption that goes beyond our understanding.

But in the waiting, in the in-between, we need grace.

Paul himself understood this need deeply. In another letter, he speaks of a *thorn in the flesh*—a struggle, a hardship that he pleaded with God to remove. And yet, instead of taking it away, God responded, *"My grace is sufficient for you, for My power is made perfect in weakness"* (2 Corinthians 12:9). Paul came to understand that God's grace was not just enough to sustain him—it was enough to transform him.

We often long for God to change our circumstances, to remove the struggles, to bring immediate resolution to our pain. But sometimes, His answer is grace. Grace to endure, grace to trust, grace to find joy even in the midst of uncertainty.

God's grace does not always take away the struggle, but it gives us the strength to walk through it. It does not always remove the storm, but it anchors us within it. It is enough—not just for some things, not just in certain seasons, but in all things.

If you are in a season of waiting, of questioning, of struggling to see the good, take heart. God has not abandoned you. He has not forgotten you. He is at work, even now, in ways beyond what you can imagine. His grace is enough for today, for tomorrow, for every moment that lies ahead.

Lean into that grace. Trust that He is writing a greater story than you can see. And hold onto the promise that in all things— yes, even in this—He is working for your good.

**Prayer**

Father, I come before You with a heart that longs to trust but sometimes struggles to understand. There are moments when I cannot see the good, when the weight of life feels overwhelming, when I wonder how You are at work. But Your Word reminds me that You are always working, always weaving every moment into something beautiful. Help me to rest in that truth.

When I feel weak, let Your grace be my strength. When doubt creeps in, remind me of Your faithfulness. When I cannot yet see the full picture, help me to trust the hands of the One who holds it all. Thank You for Your love, for Your presence, and for the assurance that nothing in my life is wasted. I surrender my worries, my questions, my need for control, and I choose to rest in the truth that Your grace is enough. In Jesus' name, Amen.

**Faith-Building Action Step**

Take a moment today to reflect on a time when God worked something for good in your life, even when you couldn't see it at the time. Write it down as a reminder of His faithfulness. If you are in the midst of a difficult season, choose one area where you will trust His grace today. Whenever doubt arises, return to Romans 8:28 and declare its truth over your life—God is working, and His grace is enough.

# 21

# Holding on to Hope – (Hebrews 10:23)

S **cripture:** *"Let us hold unswervingly to the hope we profess, for He who promised is faithful."* – Hebrews 10:23

## Devotional Reflection

Hope is one of the most powerful forces in the human heart. It has the ability to sustain us through the darkest seasons, to lift our eyes beyond present struggles, and to keep us moving forward when everything inside us wants to give up. Yet, hope can also feel fragile. It is tested by disappointment, stretched by delays, and challenged when life doesn't unfold the way we expected.

There are moments when holding on to hope feels effortless—when prayers are answered, doors open, and we see clear evidence of God's hand at work. But then there are seasons when hope feels like a battle. When waiting seems endless, when hardships persist, when circumstances try to convince us that hope is nothing more than wishful thinking. It is in these moments that the words of Hebrews 10:23 call us to a deeper kind of trust: *"Let us hold unswervingly to the hope we profess, for He who promised is faithful."*

To hold on unswervingly means to cling tightly, to refuse to waver, to remain steadfast even when the winds of doubt and discouragement try to pull us away. Hope is not just an emotion; it is a decision. A daily choice to trust that what God has promised, He will fulfill.

But how do we hold on when life feels uncertain? When prayers seem unanswered? When hope itself feels like it's slipping through our fingers?

The foundation of our hope is not in circumstances, not in people, not in outcomes going the way we desire—it is in the character of God Himself. *"For He who promised is faithful."* This is the reason we can hope, the reason we can trust, the reason we can stand firm even when everything around us is shifting. Hope is not based on what we see but on who God is.

God's faithfulness is woven throughout Scripture, a thread that runs through the lives of those who dared to believe in His promises even when everything seemed to be against them. Abraham held onto hope when God promised him a son, even though years passed without an answer. Joseph clung to hope through betrayal, slavery, and imprisonment, believing that God's plan for him was greater than his current suffering. Hannah, barren and heartbroken, poured her hope into God's faithfulness, trusting that He saw her pain.

Their stories remind us that hope is not a passive thing. It is not simply wishing for the best or hoping circumstances will change. It is active. It is a faith-filled determination to trust in God's promises even when we cannot yet see their fulfillment.

Hope does not mean we won't experience hardship. It does not mean that life will be without struggles or that faith exempts us from suffering. What it does mean is that no matter what we face, we do not face it alone. It means that even in the waiting, even in the pain, even in the moments when hope feels distant, God is still working.

One of the greatest challenges in holding onto hope is the reality of waiting. We live in a world that demands immediacy, where delays feel like detours and waiting feels like wasted time. But God's timing is not our timing. Sometimes the waiting is part of the work He is doing in us. It is in these seasons that we must remind ourselves: just because we do not see the fulfillment of His promises yet does not mean He has forgotten them.

Waiting is not a sign of abandonment. It is often the place where faith is deepened, where trust is refined, where hope is strengthened. It is in the waiting that we learn to rely on God, not just for what He can give, but for who He is.

If hope were easy, we would not need to be reminded to hold onto it. The very fact that Scripture calls us to *hold unswervingly* means that there will be moments when hope is tested. There will be days when doubt whispers that maybe God has forgotten us. There will be times when circumstances tempt us to loosen our grip.

But hope is worth holding onto, because the One who holds us is faithful.

When Jesus walked the earth, He carried a hope that defied the world's understanding. He knew suffering was ahead of Him. He knew the cross was coming. And yet, He endured *for the joy set before Him* (Hebrews 12:2). His hope was anchored in something greater—something eternal.

That same hope is ours today. A hope that is not dependent on what we feel, but on what we know to be true. A hope that is not shaken by trials, but strengthened by them. A hope that does not waver, because it is rooted in the unchanging faithfulness of God.

Maybe today, you are struggling to hold onto hope. Maybe the waiting has been long, the journey exhausting, the prayers unanswered. Maybe you are wondering if hope is even worth it anymore.

If that is where you find yourself, hear this: You are not alone. God sees you. He knows your struggles. He understands the weight you are carrying. And He is still faithful.

Hold on. Even when it's hard. Even when doubt creeps in. Even when you cannot yet see how He is working. Hold on because He who promised is faithful.

Hope is not fragile when it is placed in the hands of a faithful

God. It is unshakable, immovable, enduring. It is the anchor for our souls, securing us through every storm. And when the fulfillment of His promises finally comes, we will see that every moment of holding on, every prayer lifted in faith, every tear shed in the waiting—it was all worth it.

## Prayer

Father, in moments of doubt, remind me of Your faithfulness. When hope feels distant, draw me closer to You. Give me the strength to hold onto hope, not because of what I see, but because of who You are. Strengthen my heart in the waiting. Teach me to trust in Your timing, knowing that every promise You have spoken will come to pass. Thank You that I am never alone, that I am always held in Your love, and that my hope in You will never be in vain. In Jesus' name, Amen.

## Faith-Building Action Step

Take a moment today to write down one promise from God that you are holding onto. Place it somewhere visible as a daily reminder that He who promised is faithful. Each time doubt arises, declare His faithfulness over your situation and choose to hold onto hope.

# 22

# Joy in the Midst of Hardship – (Nehemiah 8:10)

S**cripture:** *"Do not grieve, for the joy of the Lord is your strength."* – Nehemiah 8:10

### Devotional Reflection

Hardship has a way of draining joy from the soul. When we walk through seasons of difficulty—when life feels heavy, when burdens seem unrelenting, when uncertainty looms—it can be hard to grasp the concept of joy. Joy feels like a distant memory, something reserved for times of laughter, ease, and celebration, not for moments of struggle. Yet, Scripture presents a different truth: *"Do not grieve, for the joy of the Lord is your strength."*

The words of Nehemiah 8:10 were spoken to the people of Israel at a time when they were rebuilding, restoring, and repenting. They had returned from exile, gathered together to hear the Word of God, and as the Law was read, they were overwhelmed with sorrow for how far they had fallen. Their hearts ached with conviction, their spirits burdened with the weight of past mistakes. It was in this moment, when grief and heaviness could have consumed them, that Nehemiah spoke these profound words—words that redirected their focus from sorrow to strength, from despair to joy.

The joy of the Lord is not a fleeting happiness dependent on circumstances. It is not found in external comforts or momentary pleasures. It is not something we muster up within ourselves. This joy is something deeper—something unshakable. It is a joy that comes from knowing who God is, from trusting His promises, from walking in His presence even when life is hard. It is a joy that sustains, that strengthens, that carries us when we feel like we cannot go on.

But how can joy and hardship coexist? How do we find joy when we are walking through grief, through loss, through seasons of uncertainty? The answer lies in understanding where our joy comes from.

If our joy is rooted in circumstances, then when those circumstances shift, our joy will vanish. If our joy is based on people, then when relationships change or disappoint, our joy will fade. If our joy depends on earthly success, financial stability, or personal achievements, then the moment those things are shaken, our joy will crumble. But when our joy is in the Lord, it remains steady. It is not dependent on what is happening around us, but on the One who is with us in every situation.

Jesus Himself embodied this truth. In His final hours before the cross, He spoke of joy. He told His disciples, *"I have told you this so that my joy may be in you and that your joy may be complete"* (John 15:11). Even knowing the suffering that lay ahead, He spoke of joy—because His joy was rooted in the Father, not in the absence of pain.

Paul, too, understood this reality. Sitting in a prison cell, uncertain of his future, he wrote to the Philippians, *"Rejoice in the Lord always. I will say it again: Rejoice!"* (Philippians 4:4). This was not denial of hardship; it was defiance against despair. It was a declaration that joy was not dictated by chains, by circumstances, or by suffering, but by the unchanging nature of God.

Maybe today, joy feels out of reach. Maybe life has worn you down, and the thought of rejoicing seems impossible. But hear this truth: Joy is not about ignoring pain; it is about recognizing that God is present in it. It is not about pretending everything is fine; it is about knowing that even in the midst of struggle, God is still working, still faithful, still good.

Joy is a weapon. The enemy would love nothing more than for hardship to steal your joy, for difficulties to silence your praise, for trials to convince you that there is no reason to rejoice. But joy is an act of faith. When you choose joy in the midst of hardship, you are declaring that your trust is in God, not in circumstances. You are standing firm in the truth that He is your strength, even when you feel weak.

Choosing joy does not mean denying hardship, but it does mean refusing to let hardship define you. It means looking beyond what you feel in the moment and holding onto the eternal hope that God is with you. It means finding moments of gratitude even in the midst of struggle. It means fixing your eyes on the promises of God, rather than the weight of the trial.

There will be days when joy feels distant, when weariness threatens to overwhelm, when burdens feel too heavy to bear. In those moments, remember: The joy of the Lord is not just an encouragement—it is strength. It is the very thing that will sustain you, carry you, and uphold you through every storm.

And one day, when you look back on this season, you will see that joy was not just something to be found at the end of the struggle—it was with you all along, strengthening you, sustaining you, drawing you closer to the heart of God.

**Prayer**

Father, I come before You today with a heart that longs for joy but often feels weighed down by the struggles of life. In moments of hardship, remind me that joy is not found in circumstances but in You. Help me to fix my eyes on Your faithfulness, to trust that You are working even when I cannot see it, and to find strength in Your presence. Fill me with a joy that cannot be shaken, a joy that carries me through every trial. Thank You that I do not have to walk through hardship alone, and that Your joy is my strength. In Jesus' name, Amen.

**Faith-Building Action Step**

Take a moment today to reflect on one thing that brings you joy—not because of circumstances, but because of who God is. Write it down, speak it aloud, and choose to focus on that joy in the midst of whatever challenges you are facing. Let the joy of the Lord be your strength today.

# 23

# Faith That Moves Mountains – (Matthew 17:20)

**S**cripture: *"Truly I tell you, if you have faith as small as a mustard seed, you can say to this mountain, 'Move from here to there,' and it will move. Nothing will be impossible for you."* – Matthew 17:20

## Devotional Reflection

Faith is powerful. It is the bridge between what we see and what we believe, between the natural and the supernatural, between impossibility and the miraculous. It is the foundation of our relationship with God, the very thing that keeps us walking forward even when we cannot yet see the outcome. But faith is not always easy. It is tested in the waiting, refined in the struggle, and challenged when circumstances seem immovable.

When Jesus spoke the words recorded in Matthew 17:20, He was addressing His disciples, who had just failed to cast out a demon from a boy. Confused and frustrated, they came to Jesus, asking why their prayers had not been effective. His response was both simple and profound: *"Because you have so little faith."* Then He told them something extraordinary—that even faith as small as a mustard seed could move mountains.

A mustard seed is tiny, almost insignificant in appearance. And yet, Jesus used it to illustrate a faith that carries extraordinary power. This tells us something important: It is not the size of our faith that matters, but the One in whom our faith is placed. Even the smallest faith, when rooted in God, has the power to bring about the impossible.

There are mountains we all face—circumstances that seem unmovable, struggles that feel insurmountable, prayers that appear unanswered. At times, our faith wavers because the mountain before us looks too big, too strong, too permanent. We wonder if our prayers are making a difference, if God is truly listening, if anything will ever change.

But Jesus did not say, *If you have faith as large as a mountain, you can move a mountain.* No, He said *faith as small as a mustard seed* is enough. Because it is not the greatness of our faith that moves mountains—it is the greatness of our God. Faith is not about striving to believe harder; it is about trusting deeper.

Faith that moves mountains is not a faith that never doubts, but a faith that refuses to quit. It is the kind of faith that stands firm even when the mountain does not move right away. It is a faith that keeps praying, keeps trusting, keeps declaring God's promises, even when nothing seems to be changing.

Abraham had this kind of faith. When God promised him a son, he was already an old man, and as the years passed without a child, it would have been easy to give up. But Scripture tells us that *"against all hope, Abraham in hope believed"* (Romans 4:18). His faith was not in what he could see, but in the faithfulness of the One who had made the promise. And in God's perfect timing, the promise was fulfilled.

Faith that moves mountains also requires persistence. In Luke 18, Jesus told a parable about a persistent widow who kept bringing her request before a judge until he finally granted her justice. Jesus used this story to encourage us to *keep praying and not give up* (Luke 18:1). Faith does not give up when the answer is delayed. Faith keeps pressing in, keeps knocking, keeps believing, because it knows that God is faithful.

Sometimes, faith moves mountains immediately. Other times, faith moves us while we wait for the mountain to move. There are moments when God answers prayers in an instant, changing circumstances in ways we never expected. But there are also seasons when the mountain does not move as quickly as we would like. In those times, faith strengthens us, sustains us, and transforms us, teaching us to trust God in the process.

Faith does not always look like confidence; sometimes it looks like holding on when everything in you wants to let go. It looks like Peter stepping out of the boat, walking on water toward Jesus, even though fear threatened to pull him under. It looks like the woman who had been bleeding for twelve years, pressing through the crowd just to touch the hem of Jesus' robe, believing that He could heal her. It looks like Joshua marching around Jericho for seven days, trusting that God would bring the walls down even when nothing happened at first.

Faith that moves mountains is not about having all the answers; it is about trusting the One who does. It is about surrendering our fears, our doubts, and our need to control the outcome, and instead choosing to believe that God is able.

Maybe today, you are facing a mountain that seems immovable. Maybe you have been praying for something for a long time, and the answer has not yet come. Maybe you feel like your faith is too small, too weak, too fragile.

But hear this truth: Your faith is not in vain. God sees you. He hears your prayers. And even the smallest seed of faith, when placed in His hands, can move what seems impossible.

So do not lose heart. Keep believing. Keep praying. Keep trusting that the One who spoke the universe into existence, the One who parted the Red Sea, the One who conquered death itself—is still moving mountains today.

## Prayer

Father, I come before You today with the mountains in my life— the struggles that feel too big, the prayers that feel unanswered, the situations that seem impossible. Help me to trust that even faith as small as a mustard seed is enough when it is placed in You. Strengthen my heart when doubt creeps in. Teach me to persevere in faith, to keep believing even when I cannot yet see the answer. I know that You are faithful, that You are able, and that nothing is impossible for You. In Jesus' name, Amen.

## Faith-Building Action Step

Think of a mountain in your life—something you have been praying for, believing for, waiting for. Take a step of faith today. Speak Matthew 17:20 over your situation, declaring that with God, nothing is impossible. Keep praying, keep believing, and trust that in His perfect timing, God will move.

# 24

# Living in God's Strength – (Philippians 4:13)

S cripture: *"I can do all things through Christ who strengthens me."* – Philippians 4:13

**Devotional Reflection**

There are moments in life when our own strength fails us. When the weight of responsibilities, struggles, and unexpected challenges becomes too much to bear. When we reach the end of our own endurance and feel as though we have nothing left to give. In those moments, it is easy to feel powerless, to believe that we are too weak to keep going, too worn down to take another step. But Paul, in his letter to the Philippians, offers a truth that changes everything: *"I can do all things through Christ who strengthens me."*

This verse is often quoted in moments of victory—when we accomplish something great, overcome a challenge, or achieve a long-sought goal. But Paul wrote these words not from a place of triumph, but from a prison cell. He was not standing on a mountaintop celebrating success; he was in a season of uncertainty, hardship, and suffering. And yet, in the midst of it all, he declared that his strength did not come from his circumstances, his abilities, or his own willpower—it came from Christ.

Living in God's strength means recognizing that we were never meant to rely on our own. It is easy to fall into the trap of self-sufficiency, believing that if we just try harder, push through, or muster enough determination, we can handle whatever comes our way. But sooner or later, our own strength runs out. Human endurance has limits. There comes a point when we face something too heavy, too overwhelming, too exhausting to carry on our own. And that is where we must make a choice— do we continue striving in our own power, or do we surrender and lean into the strength of God?

The strength that God provides is not like human strength. It is not temporary or dependent on how we feel. It does not fade when we are exhausted or disappear when circumstances become difficult. God's strength is constant, unwavering, and perfectly sufficient for every need.

Paul understood this deeply. Earlier in Philippians, he spoke of learning to be content in all circumstances—whether in abundance or in lack, whether in times of blessing or in seasons of difficulty. His peace did not come from his external situation but from his internal dependence on God. This is what it means to live in God's strength—to stop measuring our ability to endure by our own capacity and instead trust in the limitless power of Christ working within us.

When we rely on our own strength, we will always reach a breaking point. But when we rely on God's strength, we find that He sustains us even in the most impossible situations. The same God who parted the Red Sea for the Israelites, who gave David victory over Goliath, who provided for Elijah in the wilderness—He is the same God who strengthens us today.

Living in God's strength does not mean we will never feel weak. It does not mean that trials will not come or that we will always feel capable. In fact, God often allows us to experience our weakness so that we can truly understand the depth of His power. Paul himself wrote, *"For when I am weak, then I am strong"* (2 Corinthians 12:10). It is in those moments of weakness—when we have nothing left to give, when we feel like we are at our breaking point—that God's strength is most evident.

There is freedom in realizing that we do not have to carry everything on our own. That we do not have to have all the answers, that we do not have to push through in our own power. The world tells us to be strong, to be independent, to rely on ourselves. But God invites us to something different. He calls us to rest in Him, to surrender our burdens, to trust that His strength is enough.

Think about a child who is too tired to walk any further. A loving parent does not scold the child for being weak or insist that they keep moving on their own. Instead, the parent picks them up, carries them, holds them close. This is the kind of strength God offers us. Not a demand that we push through on our own, but an invitation to rest in His arms, to trust that He will carry us when we can no longer carry ourselves.

Maybe today, you feel like you are at the end of your strength. Maybe the burdens you are carrying feel too heavy, the path ahead too overwhelming. Maybe you are exhausted from trying to hold everything together, from pretending to be strong when you feel anything but.

If that is where you are, know this: You do not have to do this alone. God is not asking you to summon strength from within yourself. He is offering you His own. He is inviting you to lay down your weariness, to stop striving, to lean into His presence and let Him sustain you.

True strength is not found in our ability to keep going on our own. It is found in surrender. In admitting that we are weak and allowing God's power to be made perfect in our weakness. It is found in trusting that no matter how heavy the burden, no matter how long the road, no matter how impossible the situation may seem—He is strong enough.

You can do all things through Christ. Not because of who you are, but because of who He is. Not because of your own strength, but because of His power at work in you.

So rest. Trust. Let go of the weight you were never meant to carry. And live in the strength that only He can provide.

## Prayer

Father, I come before You today feeling weary, feeling weak, feeling like I have reached the limits of my own strength. But Your Word tells me that I can do all things through Christ who strengthens me. Help me to trust in that promise. Teach me to rely on Your power instead of my own. Fill me with the strength that only You can give—the strength that sustains, that carries, that never runs out. Thank You that I do not have to do this alone, that You are with me, strengthening me every step of the way. In Jesus' name, Amen.

## Faith-Building Action Step

Take a moment to surrender whatever is weighing on you today. Speak Philippians 4:13 over your situation, declaring that you are not relying on your own strength but on the strength of Christ. Whenever you feel overwhelmed, return to this truth and remind yourself that His power is enough.

# 25

# Worshiping Through the Storm – (Psalm 42:11)

**S**cripture: *"Why, my soul, are you downcast? Why so disturbed within me? Put your hope in God, for I will yet praise Him, my Savior and my God."* – Psalm 42:11

**Devotional Reflection**

Storms have a way of testing everything within us. They come unexpectedly, shaking the foundation we thought was strong, pulling at our sense of security, and leaving us with more questions than answers. Some storms rage on the outside—circumstances that shift suddenly, losses we did not see coming, challenges that feel beyond our control. Others rage within—battles in our minds, in our hearts, in the depths of our souls where fear and doubt take root.

When we find ourselves in the middle of a storm, worship may not be our first response. Our natural instinct is often to cry out for relief, to question, to wrestle with the uncertainty. We want answers, solutions, a way out. And yet, Psalm 42:11 reminds us of a different response—*"Why, my soul, are you downcast? Why so disturbed within me? Put your hope in God, for I will yet praise Him, my Savior and my God."*

There is something powerful about those words: *I will yet praise Him.* Not *I will praise Him when this is over.* Not *I will praise Him if everything turns out the way I want.* But *I will yet praise Him*—right here, right now, even in the middle of the storm.

Worship is an act of defiance against despair. It is a declaration that no matter what is happening around us, God is still worthy. It is a choice to lift our eyes above the waves, above the questions, above the fear, and fix them on the One who holds us steady.

David, the writer of this psalm, was no stranger to storms. He faced betrayal, loss, seasons of waiting, moments of deep sorrow. And yet, in the midst of it all, he did not allow his emotions to dictate his worship. He spoke directly to his own soul, challenging it to remember who God is. *Why are you downcast? Why so disturbed? Put your hope in God.*

Sometimes, worship is not an overflow of feelings but an act of faith. There are days when singing praises comes easily—when joy is abundant, when God's presence feels tangible, when our hearts are full. But then there are days when worship is a battle. When we do not feel like lifting our hands, when the words of praise feel heavy on our lips, when everything in us wants to retreat into silence.

113

It is in those moments that worship becomes the most powerful. Because worship is not just about what we feel—it is about who God is. It is not about pretending the storm does not exist, but about choosing to trust that God is greater than the storm.

Paul and Silas understood this kind of worship. Beaten and chained in a prison cell, they had every reason to despair. But instead of giving in to hopelessness, they did something unexpected: *"About midnight Paul and Silas were praying and singing hymns to God, and the other prisoners were listening to them"* (Acts 16:25). They worshiped—not because their circumstances were good, but because their God was. And as they worshiped, something miraculous happened: chains broke, doors opened, freedom came.

Worship shifts the atmosphere. It changes our focus. It moves our eyes from the problem to the Provider, from the fear to the Father, from the storm to the Savior.

Maybe today, you feel like you are in the middle of a storm. Maybe your heart is weary, your soul feels downcast, and worship feels like the last thing you can offer. If that is where you are, know this: Worship is not about having everything figured out. It is about lifting your voice in the middle of the uncertainty and declaring that God is still faithful.

Let worship be your anchor. Let it be the place where fear loses its grip, where faith rises, where peace begins to settle in your soul. And as you lift your eyes, as you lift your voice, as you remind your heart of who God is—you will find that He has been holding you through the storm all along.

## Prayer

Father, in the middle of the storm, I choose to worship You. When my heart is heavy, when my soul feels downcast, when I do not understand, I will yet praise You. You are still good. You are still faithful. You are still in control. Lift my eyes above the waves, fill my heart with peace, and let my worship rise as a declaration that You alone are my refuge. In Jesus' name, Amen.

## Faith-Building Action Step

Set aside time today to worship, even if you do not feel like it. Put on a song of praise, lift your voice, and declare God's faithfulness. Let your worship be an act of trust, a statement of faith that He is with you, even in the storm.

# 26

# Week 4: Living with Unshaken Hope

Hope is more than just wishful thinking—it is a firm foundation in God's unfailing love. No matter what life brings, His promises remain true. This week, we will learn how to anchor ourselves in lasting hope, live with confidence in His plans, and walk forward with joy, knowing that our future is secure in Him.

# 27

# God's Timing is Perfect – (Ecclesiastes 3:11)

S cripture: *"He has made everything beautiful in its time. He has also set eternity in the human heart; yet no one can fathom what God has done from beginning to end."* – Ecclesiastes 3:11

**Devotional Reflection**

Waiting is one of the hardest things we experience as believers. We live in a world that moves fast, where instant gratification is the norm and patience often feels like an inconvenience. From small, everyday delays to long seasons of waiting for prayers to be answered, we struggle to understand why God doesn't move according to our timeline. When we are in the middle of a waiting season—whether for a breakthrough, a promise fulfilled, or simply a sense of clarity—it can feel as though time is slipping away, and with it, our hope.

Yet, Ecclesiastes 3:11 reminds us of a profound truth:  God

has made everything beautiful in its time. This verse does not say *some* things or *a few* things, but *everything*. It reassures us that there is divine order even in what seems like delay, that nothing is wasted, and that God is never late. His timing is perfect, even when it doesn't align with our expectations.

When we look at Scripture, we see that God's people have always wrestled with waiting. Abraham waited twenty-five years for the son God promised him. Joseph endured years of slavery and imprisonment before stepping into his calling. Moses spent forty years in the wilderness before leading Israel to the Promised Land. David was anointed king but waited many years before taking the throne. Each of these individuals had moments where they could have questioned God's timing, where they could have wondered if He had forgotten them. And yet, in every case, His plan unfolded exactly as it was meant to.

Waiting can feel like wasted time, but in God's hands, it is a time of preparation. What we often perceive as delays are actually seasons of refinement, where God is shaping our character, teaching us trust, and preparing us for what lies ahead. If Joseph had gone straight from his father's house to Pharaoh's palace, he wouldn't have developed the wisdom, humility, and resilience needed to lead a nation. If David had taken the throne immediately after his anointing, he wouldn't have learned the depth of reliance on God that came from his years in hiding. The waiting was not a punishment; it was part of the process.

And yet, when we are in the middle of it, waiting often feels unbearable. We cry out to God, asking, *Why is this taking so long? Have You forgotten me?* The silence can be deafening, the uncertainty unsettling. But God is never inactive in our waiting. Even when we cannot see it, He is moving. He is aligning circumstances, preparing hearts, and working behind the scenes in ways we could never imagine. Just because we do not see immediate change does not mean that God is not at work.

It is easy to trust God's timing when life is unfolding the way we expect. But faith is tested in the in-between—when we are standing in the gap between a promise and its fulfillment, when the answers are not coming, when the doors remain closed. In these moments, we must remind ourselves that delay is not denial. God does not forget His promises. What He has spoken, He will bring to pass, but in His time, not ours.

One of the greatest dangers in seasons of waiting is the temptation to take matters into our own hands. We see this in the story of Abraham and Sarah. God had promised them a son, but when years passed without a sign of fulfillment, they decided to act on their own. Sarah gave her servant Hagar to Abraham, and the result was heartache, division, and consequences that lasted for generations. This is what happens when we rush ahead of God—when we try to force what is meant to be received in faith.

Trusting in God's timing requires surrender. It means releasing our grip on control, choosing to believe that He sees what we do not, and resting in the assurance that His plans are always better than ours. It is not easy. There will be days when impatience creeps in, when doubt whispers that maybe we need to act now, when fear tells us that if we wait too long, we might miss our opportunity. But God is never in a hurry, and He is never late. When the time is right, He will open the door, and no force on earth will be able to keep it shut.

Jesus Himself lived with a deep awareness of divine timing. Throughout His ministry, He often said, *"My hour has not yet come."* He understood that there was a set time for everything— His miracles, His teachings, His ultimate sacrifice. He did not rush ahead, nor did He lag behind. He moved in step with the Father, trusting that every moment was unfolding exactly as it should.

When we struggle with waiting, we must remind ourselves of the bigger picture. Ecclesiastes 3:11 tells us that God has set eternity in our hearts, yet we cannot fathom His full plan. This means that our perspective is limited. We see only a fragment of the story, while He sees the entire masterpiece. We focus on the immediate, while He is working for the eternal. If we could see things from His viewpoint, we would understand why certain doors must remain closed for now, why some answers must wait, and why His "not yet" is actually a blessing in disguise.

God's timing is not only perfect—it is also personal. He knows exactly what we need and when we need it. He is not withholding blessings out of cruelty, but out of love. Sometimes, what we desire is good, but we are not yet ready to receive it. Other times, what we are asking for is far less than what He has planned for us, and He is preparing something greater. Either way, we can rest in the truth that He is faithful.

So, how do we wait well? We wait with expectation, believing that God is at work. We wait with trust, refusing to let impatience lead us down the wrong path. We wait with worship, knowing that even in the waiting, He is worthy of our praise. And we wait with hope, confident that the One who holds time itself will make everything beautiful in its season.

If you find yourself in a waiting season today, do not lose heart. God has not forgotten you. He sees you. He knows your desires, your prayers, your tears. And He is working, even now, to bring about His perfect plan in His perfect time. Hold onto hope. Trust in His faithfulness. And know that when the time is right, what He has prepared for you will be more beautiful than anything you could have imagined.

**Prayer**

Father, I come before You today with a heart that wrestles with waiting. There are moments when it feels like time is slipping away, when I wonder if You have forgotten the desires of my heart. But Your Word reminds me that You make everything beautiful in its time. Help me to trust in Your perfect timing, to release my need for control, and to rest in the assurance that You are always at work.

When impatience creeps in, strengthen my faith. When doubt whispers that nothing is changing, remind me that You are still moving. When fear tempts me to take matters into my own hands, fill me with peace to wait on You. I believe that what You have planned is greater than what I could ever imagine, and I choose to trust You.

Thank You for being a God who sees me, who loves me, and who is always faithful. I surrender my timeline to You and ask that You would teach me to wait well. In Jesus' name, Amen.

**Faith-Building Action Step**

Take a moment today to reflect on a time in your life when God's timing proved to be perfect. Write it down as a reminder of His faithfulness. If you are in a season of waiting, choose a promise from Scripture that speaks to God's perfect timing and place it somewhere you will see it daily. Each time you feel anxious about the future, speak that promise aloud and remind yourself that God is in control.

# 28

# Walking in Daily Faith – (Galatians 2:20)

**S**cripture: *"I have been crucified with Christ and I no longer live, but Christ lives in me. The life I now live in the body, I live by faith in the Son of God, who loved me and gave Himself for me."* – Galatians 2:20

**Devotional Reflection**

Faith is not just for the extraordinary moments in life—the times when we face overwhelming challenges or stand at a crossroads requiring divine intervention. Faith is meant to be a daily journey, woven into the fabric of our lives, guiding our steps, shaping our decisions, and drawing us into deeper dependence on Christ. Galatians 2:20 speaks to this kind of faith—a faith that transforms us from the inside out, defining the way we live, not just in moments of crisis, but in the quiet, ordinary moments of each day.

Paul's words in this verse are profound: *"I have been crucified with Christ and I no longer live, but Christ lives in me."* This is the essence of what it means to walk in daily faith—it is not merely about believing in Jesus, but about surrendering completely to Him. It is recognizing that our old way of life, driven by self-reliance, fear, and striving, has been put to death, and that our new life is found in Christ alone. Faith is not just something we hold onto; it is the very foundation upon which we live.

But what does it actually mean to live by faith in the Son of God? For many of us, faith is something we associate with major life events—trusting God when we are facing financial struggles, believing for healing in the midst of sickness, relying on His strength during seasons of uncertainty. And while faith certainly carries us through these pivotal moments, its true power is revealed in the way we walk with God each and every day.

Walking in daily faith means trusting God in the ordinary, unseen places of life. It is waking up each morning with the awareness that we are not navigating this day alone. It is inviting Him into every decision, whether big or small. It is choosing to believe in His promises, even when circumstances seem unchanged. It is living with the confidence that Christ is not just an occasional helper, but the very source of our strength, wisdom, and direction.

Yet, if we are honest, living by faith daily is not always easy. We are constantly pulled in different directions—by our responsibilities, our emotions, our doubts. Some days, faith feels strong, like an unshakable anchor in our hearts. Other days, it feels distant, like we are stumbling forward without clear direction. The reality is, faith is not about feelings; it is about trust. It is about choosing, moment by moment, to depend on God even when we don't feel His presence, even when answers seem slow in coming, even when the path ahead is unclear.

Think of a child learning to walk. At first, their steps are wobbly, uncertain. They reach out for something to hold onto, seeking balance and security. But as they continue to walk, their confidence grows. They learn that even if they stumble, they are not abandoned. This is how God teaches us to walk in faith—step by step, day by day, guiding us, steadying us, reminding us that we are never alone.

Walking in faith also requires surrender. Paul says, *"The life I now live in the body, I live by faith in the Son of God."* This is not just a poetic statement—it is a call to relinquish control. Our natural tendency is to hold onto the steering wheel of our lives, to rely on our own understanding, to chart our own course. But faith asks us to let go, to trust that God's ways are higher than ours, that His plans are better, that He sees what we cannot. It is a daily decision to submit our desires, our worries, and our future into His hands.

There is a kind of freedom that comes with this surrender. When we no longer have to carry the weight of figuring everything out on our own, when we stop striving to control outcomes, we find rest. We begin to live with an open-handed trust, knowing that God is directing our steps. This does not mean that life will always be easy, that we will always understand what He is doing, or that we will never experience hardship. But it does mean that we are anchored in something greater than ourselves.

Faith is also about endurance. The journey of walking with God is not a sprint; it is a lifelong commitment. There will be seasons of waiting, times of testing, moments when we wonder if we are truly moving forward. But the beauty of faith is that it is not measured by how fast we run, but by our willingness to keep going. Even when progress seems slow, even when prayers seem unanswered, even when doubts arise, we continue walking—because we trust the One who walks beside us.

One of the most powerful examples of daily faith in Scripture is found in the story of the Israelites in the wilderness. For forty years, they depended on God for manna each morning. He did not give them a month's supply all at once; He gave them just enough for that day. This was intentional. God was teaching them that faith is not about stockpiling security, but about trusting Him one day at a time. The same is true for us. God may not show us the full picture of what lies ahead, but He gives us what we need for today. And when tomorrow comes, He will be faithful then too.

Living by faith in the Son of God also means living with love. Paul reminds us that Christ *"loved me and gave Himself for me."* Our faith is not rooted in abstract belief; it is grounded in the love of Jesus. When we truly grasp how deeply we are loved, our faith becomes more than just obedience—it becomes a response to that love. We walk in faith not because we have to, but because we trust the One who laid down His life for us.

We trust that He is good, that He is for us, that His plans are filled with hope.

Perhaps today, you feel weary in your faith. Maybe the weight of life has made you hesitant to trust, or perhaps you have been walking this journey for so long that you feel exhausted. If that is where you are, hear this: You do not have to muster up faith on your own. Christ lives in you. His strength is within you. The same power that raised Him from the dead is at work in your life. You are not walking alone.

Faith is not about having every answer. It is not about being fearless every moment. It is about taking the next step, even when you don't know where the path leads. It is about choosing to trust, even when trust feels difficult. It is about believing that God is with you, guiding you, providing for you, shaping you.

So, as you step into today, choose faith. Not just for the big things, but for the small ones too. Trust Him in the waiting, in the uncertainty, in the ordinary. Let your faith be more than just words—let it be the way you live, the way you love, the way you surrender. Walk in the confidence that Christ is in you, leading you forward, step by step, day by day.

**Prayer**

Father, I thank You that I do not have to walk this journey alone. You are with me in every step, in every moment, in every season. Teach me to live by faith, not just in the extraordinary, but in the everyday. Help me to trust You with my decisions, my uncertainties, my desires. When fear tries to creep in, remind me that You are my foundation. When doubt whispers that I am alone, remind me that You are always near.

I surrender my plans to You. I choose to walk by faith, believing that You are leading me, strengthening me, and providing for me. Thank You for Your love, for Your presence, for the assurance that I can trust You completely. May my life be a reflection of the faith I have in You. In Jesus' name, Amen.

## Faith-Building Action Step

Today, take a moment to pause and invite God into your daily routine. As you go about your tasks, whisper a prayer of trust, asking Him to guide your steps. If you find yourself worrying about the future, remind yourself of Galatians 2:20 and declare that you are living by faith in the Son of God. Let this be the foundation of your day, the confidence that shapes your choices, and the peace that carries you forward.

# 29

# Trusting God's Plan – (Jeremiah 29:11)

**S**cripture: *"For I know the plans I have for you," declares the Lord, "plans to prosper you and not to harm you, plans to give you hope and a future." –* Jeremiah 29:11

**Devotional Reflection**

Trusting God's plan is one of the most difficult yet essential aspects of walking in faith. Life has a way of taking unexpected turns, leading us through seasons of uncertainty, disappointment, and waiting. We long for clear direction, for answers that bring comfort, for a roadmap that shows us exactly where we are headed. Yet, more often than not, God asks us to trust Him without giving us the full picture.

Jeremiah 29:11 is one of the most quoted verses in Scripture, a promise that God's plans for us are good. It is a verse that brings reassurance, especially in moments of uncertainty. But to fully grasp the depth of this promise, we must look at the context in which it was spoken. These words were given to the Israelites while they were in exile—a time of hardship, separation, and longing for home. They had been uprooted from everything familiar, living in a foreign land, wondering if they would ever see restoration. God's promise did not immediately remove their suffering, nor did it provide them with an instant escape. Instead, it assured them that even in their exile, He had a plan. Even in their pain, He was working for their good.

This is the essence of faith—believing in the goodness of God's plan even when we do not understand it. There are moments in life when things do not make sense, when doors close unexpectedly, when prayers seem unanswered. In these moments, it is easy to question whether God is really in control. We may wonder why certain opportunities pass us by, why dreams are delayed, why hardship lingers longer than we would like. But the truth of Jeremiah 29:11 remains: God's plans are not to harm us. They are to give us a future and a hope.

Trusting God's plan requires surrender. It means letting go of our need to figure everything out and choosing to believe that His wisdom far exceeds our understanding. So often, we try to take control, attempting to force things to happen in our own timing. We convince ourselves that if we just work harder, plan better, or push forward more aggressively, we can shape our own destiny. But God invites us to a different way—a way of trust, of rest, of yielding our desires to His perfect will.

Consider the story of Joseph. As a young man, he had dreams of greatness, visions of a future where he would lead and be honored. Yet, before he saw those dreams fulfilled, he endured betrayal, slavery, false accusations, and imprisonment. If ever there was a moment to doubt God's plan, it was in the darkness of that prison cell. But Joseph's story reminds us that what may seem like detours are often part of God's divine design. Every trial, every setback, every moment of waiting was positioning him for the place God had prepared. And when the time was right, Joseph stepped into the fulfillment of God's promise, not as a broken man, but as one who had been refined by trust.

It is easy to trust God's plan when life is going smoothly. When doors open, when blessings flow, when everything aligns effortlessly, faith feels natural. But real trust is forged in the waiting seasons, in the moments when nothing seems to be going according to plan. It is in these times that we must remind ourselves that just because we do not see God working does not mean He is not moving. His hand is always at work, orchestrating things in ways beyond our comprehension.

God's plan is not just about where He is taking us, but about who we are becoming along the way. If the goal was simply to arrive at the destination, He could get us there instantly. But He is more interested in shaping our hearts, refining our character, and teaching us to trust Him fully. The waiting, the detours, the unexpected twists—they are not obstacles, but part of the journey He is leading us through.

The Israelites struggled with trust as they journeyed through the wilderness. Though God had delivered them from slavery, parted the Red Sea, and provided for them daily, they constantly questioned His plan. They wanted immediate answers, quick solutions, a straight path to the Promised Land. And yet, their journey was prolonged not because God had abandoned them, but because He was teaching them to rely on Him. Their impatience led to frustration, but God's faithfulness remained unchanged.

How often do we act the same way? When things do not go as expected, we assume God has forgotten us. When a prayer is not answered in the way we hoped, we wonder if He is even listening. But the reality is, His silence is not His absence. He is working, even when we cannot see it.

One of the greatest challenges in trusting God's plan is releasing our own expectations. We often have a picture of how we think our lives should unfold—specific timelines, dreams we want fulfilled, paths we expect to walk. When things do not align with our vision, disappointment creeps in. But true faith means laying down our plans and embracing the truth that His ways are higher than ours. What we see as delays, He sees as preparation. What we view as setbacks, He uses as setups for something greater.

Jesus Himself demonstrated the ultimate trust in the Father's plan. In the Garden of Gethsemane, facing the cross, He prayed, *"Father, if You are willing, take this cup from me; yet not my will, but Yours be done."* (Luke 22:42). Even in agony, He surrendered to the perfect plan of God. And through that surrender, redemption was brought to the world.

Maybe today, you are in a season where trusting God's plan feels difficult. Perhaps you are waiting for an answer, longing for a breakthrough, or struggling to understand why things have unfolded the way they have. If that is you, take heart.

God's plans are still good. He is not finished writing your story. He is not withholding His best from you—He is preparing you for it.

Trust does not mean we will always have clarity. It does not mean that the road ahead will be free of obstacles. But it does mean that we can walk forward in peace, knowing that we are held by a God who sees the end from the beginning. His timing is perfect. His ways are good. And His plans will always lead us to a future filled with hope.

## Prayer

Father, I come before You today, surrendering my plans, my expectations, and my uncertainties into Your hands. You know the desires of my heart, the dreams I long to see fulfilled, the questions that weigh on my mind. Yet, Your Word reminds me that Your plans for me are good, that You are leading me toward a future filled with hope.

Help me to trust You even when I do not understand. When things do not go as expected, remind me that You are still in control. When impatience creeps in, teach me to wait on You. When fear tries to take hold, fill me with the peace that comes from knowing You are working in ways beyond what I can see.

I choose to trust that You are ordering my steps. I choose to believe that nothing is wasted in Your hands. I release my need for control and rest in the assurance that Your plans are far greater than my own. Thank You for Your faithfulness, for Your goodness, and for the promise that You are always leading me toward Your perfect will. In Jesus' name, Amen.

## Faith-Building Action Step

Take a moment today to reflect on a time when God's plan turned out to be better than what you had originally hoped for. Write it down as a reminder of His faithfulness. If you are currently in a season of waiting, pray over Jeremiah 29:11 and choose to surrender your plans to God. Each time doubt or worry creeps in, speak this promise over your life, declaring that God's plans for you are good, and He is leading you into a future filled with hope.

# 30

# Love That Casts Out Fear – (1 John 4:18)

S**cripture:** *"There is no fear in love. But perfect love drives out fear, because fear has to do with punishment. The one who fears is not made perfect in love."* – 1 John 4:18

**Devotional Reflection**

Fear is a powerful force. It sneaks into our thoughts, shaping our decisions and influencing how we see the world. It holds us back from stepping into the fullness of life God has for us, whispering lies that keep us trapped in worry, insecurity, and doubt. At its worst, fear paralyzes us, making us believe that we are alone, unprotected, and without hope.

Yet, 1 John 4:18 speaks a greater truth—one that has the power to set us free. *"There is no fear in love. But perfect love drives out fear."* These words are more than just comfort; they are a divine reality. The love of God is not just an emotion or an abstract concept—it is an active force, a light that overcomes darkness, a presence that overpowers fear at its very core.

From the moment sin entered the world, fear followed close behind. In the Garden of Eden, when Adam and Eve disobeyed God, their first reaction was to hide. Shame and fear took hold of them, convincing them that they needed to run from the very One who had created them in love. That same pattern repeats in our own lives. When we make mistakes, when we feel inadequate, when life feels out of control, fear tells us to retreat, to build walls, to live cautiously. But God's love invites us to something greater—to step out of fear and into the safety of His presence.

Fear and love cannot coexist. Where one is present, the other is absent. This is why John tells us that *perfect love drives out fear*. It does not simply calm fear or quiet it for a moment—it removes it completely. But what is this perfect love? It is the love of God, the love that sent Jesus to the cross, the love that reaches into our darkest places and declares, *You are mine. You are safe. You are fully known and fully loved.*

Many of us struggle with fear because we have not fully grasped the depth of God's love. We believe in Him, yet we still feel the need to control our own lives, to protect ourselves from disappointment, to hold onto anxieties as if they offer some form of security. But fear thrives in uncertainty, while love thrives in trust. When we truly understand the love of God—not just intellectually, but deep in our hearts—fear loses its grip.

Consider Peter walking on water. As long as his eyes were

fixed on Jesus, he moved forward in faith. But the moment he looked at the wind and the waves, fear took hold, and he began to sink. The storm did not change; it had been there all along. What changed was his focus. Fear grew the moment he shifted his gaze from Jesus to his circumstances. The same is true for us. When we dwell on what could go wrong, when we let anxious thoughts take over, fear grows. But when we focus on the perfect love of God, fear is cast out.

Fear tells us that we are not enough, that we must work harder, be stronger, do more. But God's love says, *Come as you are.* Fear tells us that if we fail, we will be rejected. But God's love says, *Nothing can separate you from My love.* Fear tells us that we are alone in our struggles. But God's love says, *I am with you always.*

One of the most crippling fears we face is the fear of the unknown. We long for certainty, for guarantees that things will turn out the way we hope. But walking in faith means trusting that God's love is greater than any uncertainty. It means believing that no matter what happens, we are held securely in His hands. We do not have to have every answer, because we have the One who is the answer.

The love of God is not like human love. It is not conditional, nor does it waver based on our actions. It is steady, unchanging, relentless. When we fail, it remains. When we doubt, it persists. When we feel unworthy, it surrounds us all the more. This is the love that casts out fear—not a weak or passive love, but a perfect, unstoppable love that conquers every lie, every doubt, every insecurity.

There are moments when fear will still try to creep in. The enemy knows that if he can keep us afraid, he can keep us from fully experiencing the life God has for us. But when fear arises, we must confront it with truth. Instead of allowing anxious thoughts to take root, we remind ourselves of who God is. He is our protector, our provider, our refuge. His love is not distant; it is near. It is within us, surrounding us, going before us.

Imagine a child in the arms of a loving parent. No matter what is happening around them, they feel safe. The presence of love removes fear. They do not have to understand everything; they simply trust in the one holding them. That is the picture of our relationship with God. His love is the place where fear has no power.

Perhaps today, you are carrying fears that have weighed you down for far too long. Maybe fear has held you back from stepping into God's calling for your life. Maybe it has kept you from opening your heart fully, from walking in confidence, from believing that you are truly loved. If that is you, hear this: You were not created to live in fear. You were created to live in love.

God is inviting you to lay down every fear at His feet—to surrender every worry, every anxious thought, every uncertainty—and to step into the freedom of His love. Fear may have whispered lies, but love speaks truth. Fear may have held you back, but love calls you forward. Fear may have seemed powerful, but love is greater.

The more we abide in God's love, the more fear loses its

hold. The more we trust in who He is, the more we walk in confidence. His love is our refuge, our foundation, our constant assurance that we are never alone.

No matter what you are facing, no matter what unknowns lie ahead, one thing is certain: You are loved by a God who is bigger than any fear. And His perfect love is casting out every shadow, breaking every chain, and calling you into a life of bold, unshaken hope.

**Prayer**

Father, I come before You with every fear, every doubt, every anxious thought that has tried to take hold of my heart. Your Word tells me that Your perfect love casts out all fear. I choose today to rest in that love. I surrender my worries, my uncertainties, my need for control, and I place them in Your hands.

Help me to trust in Your love more deeply. When fear tries to creep in, remind me that I am safe in You. When anxiety threatens to overwhelm me, let Your peace wash over me. Teach me to fix my eyes on You, knowing that I do not walk this journey alone.

Thank You for a love that is greater than my fears, stronger than my doubts, and constant in every season. Let my heart be anchored in this truth, and let my life reflect the confidence that comes from knowing I am fully known and fully loved. In Jesus' name, Amen.

## Faith-Building Action Step

Take a moment today to identify one fear that has been holding you back. Bring it before God in prayer and declare 1 John 4:18 over it. Write down the truth that God's love is greater than that fear, and place it somewhere you can see it daily. Each time fear tries to return, remind yourself that you are covered in the perfect love of God, and in that love, fear has no power.

# 31

# The Power of Gratitude – (1 Thessalonians 5:16-18)

**S**cripture: *"Rejoice always, pray continually, give thanks in all circumstances; for this is God's will for you in Christ Jesus." –* 1 Thessalonians 5:16-18

**Devotional Reflection**

Gratitude is one of the most powerful spiritual practices we can cultivate. It has the ability to shift our perspective, strengthen our faith, and bring peace to our hearts, even in the midst of uncertainty. But true gratitude is not just about giving thanks when life is going well—it is about maintaining a heart of thanksgiving in *all* circumstances. This is the challenge Paul sets before us in 1 Thessalonians 5:16-18: *Rejoice always, pray continually, and give thanks in all circumstances.* These words are not mere suggestions; they reveal a deep truth about the nature of faith and the power of gratitude.

Gratitude is a choice. It is not dependent on emotions, nor is it reserved for moments when everything in life feels aligned. Rather, it is an intentional act of faith—a decision to recognize the goodness of God regardless of the circumstances we find ourselves in. This does not mean we deny hardship or pretend that struggles do not exist. Instead, it means we choose to focus on what is unchanging: the faithfulness of God, His love for us, and the hope we have in Him.

In times of blessing, gratitude comes naturally. When prayers are answered, when doors open, when joy fills our hearts, thanksgiving overflows easily. But what about the moments when life is difficult? When we are facing trials, when disappointment weighs on our souls, when the future seems uncertain—how do we give thanks then? This is where gratitude becomes a spiritual discipline rather than just a reaction. It is in these moments that our faith is tested, and our response to difficulty reveals the depth of our trust in God.

The Bible does not instruct us to give thanks *for* all circumstances but *in* all circumstances. There is a difference. We do not have to be thankful for pain, loss, or hardship. But even in the midst of those struggles, we can still find reasons to be grateful. We can still acknowledge God's presence, His sustaining grace, His promises that remain true even when life is hard. Gratitude in hardship is not about ignoring reality; it is about choosing to see God's hand at work even when things do not make sense.

Consider Paul and Silas in prison. They had been beaten, chained, and confined to a dark cell, yet their response was not despair—it was worship. In the midnight hour, they sang praises to God, lifting their voices in thanksgiving despite their suffering. And in that moment, something miraculous happened: the prison shook, their chains fell off, and freedom came. Their gratitude did not change their circumstances instantly, but it shifted the atmosphere. Their hearts remained focused on God rather than their suffering, and in doing so, they witnessed His power move in ways they never could have imagined.

Gratitude has the power to transform our outlook. When we fix our eyes on what is lacking, we become consumed by frustration, envy, and doubt. But when we choose to focus on what we have been given, we cultivate a heart of contentment and joy. The enemy would love nothing more than to keep us trapped in a cycle of dissatisfaction, always longing for what is next, always feeling like we are missing something. But gratitude disrupts that pattern. It reminds us that God has already provided, that we are already blessed, that we are already loved beyond measure.

Jesus demonstrated this principle throughout His ministry. Before feeding the five thousand, He gave thanks. Before raising Lazarus from the dead, He lifted His eyes and thanked the Father. Even on the night before His crucifixion, as He shared the Last Supper with His disciples, He took the bread, broke it, and *gave thanks.* Knowing what was ahead, knowing the suffering He would endure, He still chose gratitude. If Jesus could give thanks in the face of the cross, then surely we can choose gratitude in the midst of our struggles.

Gratitude also strengthens our faith. When we make a habit

of giving thanks, we begin to recognize how present God is in our lives. We see His provision in the little things, His grace in the unexpected moments, His faithfulness woven through our stories. Keeping a heart of gratitude allows us to look back and remember how God has carried us through before, which gives us confidence that He will do it again.

One of the most remarkable aspects of gratitude is its ability to bring peace. When anxiety rises, when worries fill our minds, thanksgiving serves as a remedy. Paul writes in Philippians 4:6-7, *"Do not be anxious about anything, but in every situation, by prayer and petition, with thanksgiving, present your requests to God. And the peace of God, which transcends all understanding, will guard your hearts and your minds in Christ Jesus."* Gratitude and peace are deeply connected. When we shift our focus from what we fear to what we are grateful for, our hearts settle into a place of trust. We begin to see that God is in control, that He has been faithful before, and that He will continue to be faithful now.

There will be days when gratitude feels difficult, when the weight of life makes it hard to see beyond the present struggles. In those moments, it is okay to be honest with God. We do not have to force joy or manufacture thanksgiving. But even in those times, we can take small steps—whispering a prayer of thanks for His presence, for His promises, for the breath in our lungs. Gratitude does not have to be extravagant; sometimes, it is simply the quiet acknowledgment that God is still good, even here, even now.

Perhaps today, you are facing a season where gratitude feels like a challenge. Maybe life is uncertain, and your heart feels heavy. If that is you, know this: gratitude is not about ignoring your struggles; it is about inviting God into them. It is about choosing to see Him in the middle of the unknown, to trust that He is working even when you cannot yet see the full picture. Gratitude does not mean pretending that everything is perfect—it means recognizing that God is still present, still good, still worthy of praise.

When we live with gratitude, we begin to walk in a deeper awareness of God's grace. We stop waiting for *something* to make us happy, and we realize that joy is found in what we already have: a God who loves us unconditionally, a Savior who walks with us, a Spirit who fills us with peace. The power of gratitude is not just in the words we speak but in the way it shapes our hearts. It is a posture of trust, a declaration of faith, a reminder that no matter what comes, God is still worthy of thanks.

## Prayer

Father, I thank You for the countless ways You have blessed me. In moments of joy and in moments of struggle, You are always with me. Teach me to cultivate a heart of gratitude, not just when life is easy, but in all circumstances. Help me to see Your goodness in the little things, to recognize Your hand at work even when I do not understand, and to trust that You are always faithful.

When anxiety tries to take hold, let thanksgiving be my response. When fear whispers doubt, let gratitude be my weapon. Fill my heart with the peace that comes from trusting You completely. I choose to rejoice, to pray continually, and to give thanks, knowing that Your plans for me are good and that You are always working for my good.

Thank You, Lord, for Your unending love, for the breath in my lungs, for the blessings I often overlook. Let my life be a reflection of the gratitude I have for all that You are. In Jesus' name, Amen.

## Faith-Building Action Step

Take a moment today to write down three things you are grateful for. They do not have to be grand or extraordinary—just simple reminders of God's goodness in your life. Keep this list where you can see it, and each time you feel overwhelmed, return to it. Let it be a reminder that even in the hardest seasons, there is always something to thank God for.

# 32

# Living in the Peace of Christ – (Colossians 3:15)

S**cripture:** *"Let the peace of Christ rule in your hearts, since as members of one body you were called to peace. And be thankful."* – Colossians 3:15

**Devotional Reflection**

Peace is something we all long for. In a world filled with uncertainty, stress, and constant noise, the idea of living in peace can sometimes feel impossible. We search for it in different ways—through security, stability, control, and even distraction—but true, lasting peace does not come from external circumstances. It is found in Christ alone.

Paul's words in Colossians 3:15 remind us that peace is not just something we experience occasionally; it is something we are called to *live in*. This peace is not fleeting or dependent on whether life is going according to plan. It is the peace of Christ—a supernatural, unwavering peace that transcends understanding, calms anxious hearts, and anchors us even in the midst of life's storms.

To live in the peace of Christ means to let it *rule* in our hearts. The word *rule* suggests authority, a governing force that dictates our responses and shapes our perspective. Peace is not merely an emotion or a moment of relief; it is a position of the heart, a state of being that affects how we think, how we act, and how we trust in God. When the peace of Christ rules in us, fear loses its hold, anxiety is quieted, and our hearts are steadied in His presence.

But peace is not something that happens automatically. If we are not intentional, worry and doubt will try to take its place. Our natural tendency is to let circumstances dictate our peace—to feel at rest when things are going well and to become anxious when challenges arise. Yet, Jesus offers us something far greater. In John 14:27, He says, *"Peace I leave with you; my peace I give you. I do not give to you as the world gives. Do not let your hearts be troubled and do not be afraid."* The peace that Jesus gives is different from what the world offers. It is not based on everything being perfect. It is rooted in His presence, His faithfulness, and His unchanging nature.

The world defines peace as the absence of conflict, but Christ's peace is different. It does not require perfect conditions. It is the kind of peace that allows us to stand firm even when life feels uncertain. It is the kind of peace that remains when answers are delayed, when prayers seem unanswered, when circumstances are difficult. It is the peace that was present when Jesus slept in the boat during a raging storm, while His disciples were filled with fear. The storm did not shake Him, because His peace was not tied to external conditions—it was grounded in His trust in the Father.

This same peace is available to us. But how do we walk in it daily? How do we allow it to rule in our hearts, especially when life feels anything but peaceful?

It begins with surrender. So often, we forfeit peace because we try to carry burdens that were never meant to be ours. We attempt to control outcomes, fix problems in our own strength, and predict the future instead of trusting God. But peace comes when we release our grip, when we let go of our need to control and place everything in God's hands. Philippians 4:6-7 reminds us of this: *"Do not be anxious about anything, but in every situation, by prayer and petition, with thanksgiving, present your requests to God. And the peace of God, which transcends all understanding, will guard your hearts and your minds in Christ Jesus."*

Peace is not something we manufacture; it is something we receive. It is a gift from God, given to those who choose to trust Him fully. When we take our worries to Him in prayer, when we lay down our anxieties and replace them with thanksgiving, His peace takes over. It does not always change our situation immediately, but it changes *us*—it guards our hearts, settles our minds, and fills us with confidence that He is in control.

Another key to living in the peace of Christ is fixing our minds on Him. Isaiah 26:3 says, *"You will keep in perfect peace those whose minds are steadfast, because they trust in you."* Our thoughts shape our reality. When we focus on our problems,

149

peace is replaced by stress. When we dwell on uncertainties, anxiety grows. But when we fix our minds on God—on His faithfulness, His promises, His character—peace becomes our reality.

Worship is one of the most powerful ways to shift our focus. When we praise God in the middle of our struggles, when we declare His goodness despite what we see, we create space for His peace to fill our hearts. Worship reminds us of who He is, lifting our perspective above the chaos and anchoring us in the truth that He is still on the throne.

Living in the peace of Christ also requires obedience. Sometimes, we lack peace because we are resisting what God is asking of us. We know He is calling us to step out in faith, to trust Him in a new way, but we hesitate. We hold onto our own plans, fearing what surrender might cost. But true peace is found in alignment with God's will. When we walk in obedience, even when it feels uncertain, we discover a deep, abiding peace that reassures us we are exactly where we are meant to be.

Jesus lived in perfect peace because He lived in perfect surrender to the Father. He did not rush ahead, nor did He hesitate in fear. He walked in step with God's timing, fully trusting in His plan. And because of that, He was never shaken. Even in the face of the cross, He remained in peace, knowing that His Father was in control.

Perhaps today, you find yourself longing for peace. Maybe your heart has been troubled, weighed down by worries and uncertainties. If so, hear this: Peace is not something you have to chase after; it is already yours in Christ. He has given it to you freely. All He asks is that you receive it, that you allow it to take root in your heart, that you let it rule over fear, over doubt, over everything that tries to steal your rest.

Peace does not mean life will always be easy. It does not mean there will never be storms. But it does mean that no matter what comes, you are secure in the hands of a loving, sovereign God. His peace is steady. It is unwavering. It is your inheritance as His child. And when you choose to walk in it, when you allow it to define your life, you become a reflection of Christ to the world—a living testimony of the unshaken hope that is found in Him alone.

**Prayer**

Father, I come before You with a heart that longs for Your peace. In a world filled with uncertainty, it is easy to let fear and worry take over. But Your Word tells me to let the peace of Christ rule in my heart. Today, I choose to surrender my fears to You. I release my need for control, and I place my trust fully in Your hands.

When my thoughts become anxious, remind me to fix my eyes on You. When circumstances feel overwhelming, let Your peace guard my heart. Help me to live each day anchored in the confidence that You are with me, that You are working all things for my good, and that nothing can shake me when I stand in Your presence.

Thank You for the gift of peace that surpasses understanding. Teach me to walk in it daily, to rest in Your promises, and to reflect Your peace to those around me. I trust You, Lord, and I receive Your peace today. In Jesus' name, Amen.

## Faith-Building Action Step

Set aside time today to sit quietly in God's presence. Close your eyes, take a deep breath, and surrender every worry, every fear, every burden to Him. As you do, invite His peace to fill your heart. Whenever anxious thoughts arise throughout the day, speak Colossians 3:15 over yourself and choose to let the peace of Christ rule in your heart.

# 33

# From Worry to Worship – (Psalm 28:7)

**S**cripture: *"The Lord is my strength and my shield; my heart trusts in Him, and He helps me. My heart leaps for joy, and with my song I praise Him."* – Psalm 28:7

**Devotional Reflection**

Worry has a way of creeping into our hearts, sometimes without us even realizing it. One moment, we are confident in God's goodness, trusting in His plans, standing firm in His promises. And then, with little warning, anxious thoughts begin to swirl—*What if things don't work out? What if I fail? What if the answer never comes?* Worry starts as a whisper, but if left unchecked, it can grow into a storm that consumes our minds, leaving us restless and fearful.

Yet, Scripture offers us a powerful antidote to worry—worship. Psalm 28:7 captures this beautifully: *"The Lord is my strength and my shield; my heart trusts in Him, and He helps me. My heart leaps for joy, and with my song I praise Him."* This verse reveals a profound truth: When we shift our focus from our worries to the character of God, something incredible happens—our hearts are lifted, our strength is renewed, and our spirits move from anxiety to adoration.

Worship is not just a response to good times; it is a weapon against fear. It is an act of defiance against the voice of worry that tells us we are alone, unprotected, and without hope. When we choose to worship in the midst of uncertainty, we declare that God is still in control. We remind ourselves that our strength is not found in our circumstances, but in the One who holds all things together.

David, the author of Psalm 28, knew what it meant to be overwhelmed. He faced battles, betrayals, and seasons of waiting where answers seemed distant. But through it all, he discovered the power of worship. He learned that even when life felt chaotic, he could still lift his voice in praise. His circumstances did not always change immediately, but his perspective did. Worship has a way of shifting our gaze from what is uncertain to the One who is unshakable.

When we worry, our minds become consumed with what we cannot control. We replay scenarios, search for solutions, and try to predict outcomes. But worry does not solve problems—it only magnifies them. Worship, on the other hand, does the opposite. It shifts our focus from the unknown to the known, from our fears to God's faithfulness. It reminds us that no matter what we face, God is our shield, our help, and our strength.

One of the greatest examples of moving from worry to worship is found in the life of Jehoshaphat, the king of Judah. In 2 Chronicles 20, he faced an overwhelming army that threatened to destroy his people. Fear could have overtaken him, but instead of giving in to worry, he turned to God in prayer. He did not formulate a battle strategy rooted in human wisdom; he sought the Lord. And in response, God gave him an unusual command—*send worshippers ahead of the army.* As the people of Judah sang praises to God, their enemies were thrown into confusion and defeated. Victory came not through military strength, but through worship.

This is the power of praise. Worship invites God into the battle. It is a declaration that we trust Him even when we do not see the way forward. It is an act of surrender that releases our need for control and places everything into His hands. Worship does not deny the reality of our struggles, but it places them in perspective. It reminds us that the One who spoke the universe into existence is the same One fighting for us.

But what does it look like to turn worry into worship in our daily lives? It begins with a choice. When anxious thoughts arise, we can either dwell on them or replace them with truth. When fear tries to grip our hearts, we can either let it take hold or lift our hands in surrender. Worship is not about waiting until we *feel* at peace; it is about praising God *until* peace comes.

There is something powerful about singing in the midst of uncertainty. The enemy wants us to stay silent, to let fear drown out our faith. But when we open our mouths in worship, when we declare God's goodness even when we do not see the full picture, we are aligning our hearts with heaven. The Psalms are filled with this pattern—cries of distress followed by declarations of God's faithfulness. David often began his songs with questions and concerns, but by the end, his words were filled with confidence in the Lord. This is the effect of worship—it transforms our hearts.

Think about Paul and Silas in prison. They had every reason to worry, to feel abandoned, to question why they were suffering after faithfully serving God. Yet, instead of sinking into despair, they prayed and sang hymns. And as they worshipped, something miraculous happened—the prison doors flew open, and their chains fell off. Worship not only freed them physically; it freed them spiritually. It took their focus off their situation and placed it on the power of God.

Perhaps today, you find yourself weighed down by worry. Maybe you have been carrying burdens that feel too heavy to bear. If that is you, know this: God has not called you to live in fear. He has called you to live in faith. And one of the most powerful ways to walk in faith is through worship.

Worship reminds us that we are not alone. It fills the space where anxiety once lived and replaces it with the presence of God. When we lift our voices in praise, even in the midst of struggle, we are declaring that our trust is in Him.

There will be moments when worship feels difficult. When the weight of life presses in, when the answers seem delayed, when fear whispers that nothing will change—those are the moments when worship is most needed. It is easy to praise when life is going well. But the greatest breakthroughs come when we choose to worship in the waiting, in the trials, in the moments when our hearts feel weary.

God sees you. He knows the worries that have tried to steal your peace. And He invites you into something greater—a life of worship that is not dictated by circumstances, but anchored in His faithfulness. When you feel anxious, lift your voice. When fear rises, sing of His goodness. When you do not know what to do next, declare His promises. Worship is not about pretending everything is perfect; it is about trusting that God is.

As you step into this day, let worship be your response to every worry. Let praise fill the spaces where anxiety once lived. The Lord is your strength and your shield. Your heart can trust in Him. And as you choose to worship, His peace will fill you, His presence will surround you, and joy will rise where fear once stood.

**Prayer**

Father, I come before You with every worry, every fear, every anxious thought that has weighed on my heart. I lay them at Your feet and choose to worship instead of worry. You are my strength and my shield. My heart trusts in You, and I know that You will help me.

Teach me to shift my focus from my circumstances to Your faithfulness. When fear tries to creep in, let worship rise within me. When anxiety stirs, remind me of who You are. Fill my heart with peace that surpasses understanding, and let my soul rest in the truth that You are in control.

Thank You for being my refuge, my protector, my ever-present help. I choose to worship You in the waiting, in the trials, in every season of my life. You are worthy of all my praise, and I surrender every worry into Your hands. In Jesus' name, Amen.

**Faith-Building Action Step**

Take a moment today to turn your worries into worship. Find a song that declares God's faithfulness and sing it aloud, even if you do not feel like it. Let your praise be louder than your fears. Whenever anxious thoughts try to return, respond with worship. Declare Psalm 28:7 over your life and trust that as you lift your voice in praise, God is lifting your burdens in His hands.

# 34

# Standing Firm in Faith – (Ephesians 6:13)

**S**cripture: *"Therefore put on the full armor of God, so that when the day of evil comes, you may be able to stand your ground, and after you have done everything, to stand."* – Ephesians 6:13

**Devotional Reflection**

Faith is not passive; it is active. It is not simply believing in God's existence but trusting Him enough to stand firm when trials come. Life has a way of testing what we believe. There are moments when we feel strong, unwavering in our confidence in God's promises. And then, there are moments when our faith is shaken—when circumstances challenge us, when prayers seem unanswered, when fear whispers that we are alone. It is in these moments that we must hold our ground, refusing to be moved by doubt or fear, choosing instead to stand firm in faith.

Paul's words in Ephesians 6:13 remind us that faith is not just about moving forward but also about standing firm. *"Put on the full armor of God, so that when the day of evil comes, you may be able to stand your ground."* He does not say *if* the day of evil comes, but *when*. Challenges are inevitable. Battles will come. But God has given us everything we need to stand strong, no matter what we face.

Standing firm in faith does not mean life will be free of hardship. It means that when trials come, we will not be uprooted. A tree with deep roots can withstand the fiercest storms because it is grounded. The same is true for us. When our faith is rooted in Christ, we can endure the fiercest winds of life without being shaken.

One of the greatest threats to standing firm is fear. Fear causes us to question what we once believed. It makes us wonder if God is truly with us, if His promises are still true, if we have the strength to endure. But faith is not about the absence of fear; it is about trusting God despite it. It is about choosing to believe His Word over what we see and feel.

Think of Peter walking on water. As long as his eyes were fixed on Jesus, he stood firm. But the moment he focused on the wind and the waves, he began to sink. The storm did not change—what changed was Peter's focus. The same happens in our lives. When we fix our eyes on Jesus, we stand firm. But when we allow circumstances to dictate our faith, we begin to falter.

Faith is a daily decision. It is not just something we turn

to in crisis, but something we cultivate every day. Just as a soldier prepares for battle before the war begins, we must equip ourselves spiritually so that when challenges arise, we are ready. We do this through prayer, through meditating on God's Word, through worship, and through walking in obedience.

The enemy will try to shake our faith. He will plant seeds of doubt, whisper lies, attempt to convince us that we are too weak, too broken, too far gone. But faith is not about our strength—it is about God's. When we rely on Him, when we put on the full armor of God, we are equipped to stand firm against every attack.

Paul describes this armor in detail: the belt of truth, the breastplate of righteousness, the shoes of peace, the shield of faith, the helmet of salvation, and the sword of the Spirit. Each piece is essential. Truth grounds us when the world tries to distort reality. Righteousness protects our hearts from guilt and condemnation. Peace keeps us steady when anxiety tries to take over. Faith shields us from the flaming arrows of doubt. Salvation reminds us of who we are in Christ. And the Word of God is our weapon, the truth we declare in every battle.

Faith is not about avoiding hardship; it is about enduring it with confidence in God. Shadrach, Meshach, and Abednego stood firm when faced with the fiery furnace. They did not know if God would deliver them, but they knew He was able. Their faith was not dependent on the outcome—it was rooted in who God was. That kind of faith does not waver, even in the face of fire.

161

There will be days when standing firm feels difficult. When waiting on God's timing is exhausting. When prayers seem to echo in silence. When trials feel relentless. But in those moments, remember this: You are not standing alone. The same God who parted the Red Sea, who shut the mouths of lions, who raised the dead—He is the One holding you steady.

Standing firm does not mean we will always feel strong. There will be moments when we feel weak, weary, unsure. But even in those moments, we can stand—not because of our own strength, but because of His. *"My grace is sufficient for you, for my power is made perfect in weakness."* (2 Corinthians 12:9).

God's faithfulness does not depend on our emotions. Even when we feel like our faith is small, He remains unshaken. Even when we struggle to believe, He is still working. Our job is not to have all the answers—it is to trust the One who does.

Perhaps today, you feel like you are barely holding on. Maybe the weight of life's struggles has made it hard to stand firm. If that is you, know this: God sees you. He is strengthening you even now. The battle you are facing will not destroy you. You are being refined, strengthened, prepared. And as you continue to stand, you will see His faithfulness unfold in ways you never imagined.

Standing firm in faith is not about knowing the future—it is about trusting the One who holds it. It is about believing that no matter what comes, you are secure in Him. When the storm rages, stand firm. When the enemy attacks, stand firm. When fear tries to creep in, stand firm. Because God is with you. And in Him, you are unshakable.

## Prayer

Father, I thank You for the strength to stand firm in faith. Life brings challenges, but You are greater than anything I face. When fear tries to take hold, remind me that You are my refuge. When doubt creeps in, help me to stand on Your truth.

Teach me to put on the full armor of God daily, to be rooted in Your Word, to walk in confidence, knowing that You fight for me. Strengthen my heart in times of uncertainty. When I feel weak, remind me that Your grace is enough.

I choose today to stand firm—not in my own strength, but in Yours. No matter what comes, I trust You. You are my foundation, my protector, my unshakable hope. Thank You for never leaving me, for always guiding me, for being faithful in every season. In Jesus' name, Amen.

## Faith-Building Action Step

Take time today to reflect on an area of your life where you need to stand firm in faith. Write down a promise from Scripture that speaks to your situation and declare it over your life. Each time fear or doubt tries to rise, return to that promise and remind yourself that God is your strength. Choose to stand firm, knowing that He is with you and will never let you fall.

# 35

# Hope Unshaken – (Romans 15:13)

**S**cripture: *"May the God of hope fill you with all joy and peace as you trust in Him, so that you may overflow with hope by the power of the Holy Spirit."* – Romans 15:13

**Devotional Reflection**

Hope is more than a feeling. It is more than wishful thinking or optimism. Hope is an anchor, a foundation that holds us steady when life feels uncertain. It is the quiet confidence that God is who He says He is, that His promises will come to pass, that no matter what we face, He is working all things together for good. True hope is not fragile or fleeting—it is unshaken. It is rooted in something deeper than circumstances, stronger than fear, more certain than the trials of this world.

Paul's words in Romans 15:13 remind us that our hope is not found in ourselves, in others, or in the fleeting comforts of life. It is found in God alone. He is *the God of hope*, the source from which all hope flows. And when we trust in Him, He fills us—

not just with enough hope to get by, but with an overflowing, abundant hope that transforms the way we live.

There are seasons when hope feels distant. When prayers seem unanswered, when struggles seem unending, when disappointment settles into the heart. In these moments, it can be easy to feel as though hope is slipping through our fingers, like a candle flickering in the wind. But hope that is anchored in Christ does not fade. It does not rise and fall with circumstances. It remains, steady and unwavering, because it is not built on what we see—it is built on who He is.

The enemy would love nothing more than to steal our hope. He knows that a heart filled with hope is dangerous. Hope fuels perseverance, strengthens faith, and leads us into deeper trust in God. When we hold onto hope, we refuse to be defeated by fear. We stand firm, knowing that even if we cannot see the outcome yet, God is still in control.

Hope does not mean that life will always be easy. It does not mean that we will always have clarity or that every moment will be free of struggle. But it does mean that even in uncertainty, we can rest in the promise that God is with us. It means that even in waiting, we can trust that He is working. It means that even in hardship, we can believe that He is still good.

Paul's prayer in this verse is not just for a small measure of hope—it is for overflowing hope. A hope so abundant that it spills out into every area of our lives, touching those around us, reminding the world that God is faithful. This kind of hope is not something we manufacture on our own. It is given by the Holy Spirit, a divine assurance that carries us through the darkest valleys and the longest nights.

Throughout Scripture, we see people who clung to unshaken hope despite impossible circumstances. Abraham believed God's promise of a son, even when years passed without fulfillment. Joseph held onto his dreams, even when betrayed, imprisoned, and forgotten. Hannah prayed in faith, trusting that God saw her sorrow. Their hope was not in their own ability to change their situation, but in the faithfulness of the One who had spoken.

Hope allows us to live differently. When we are filled with the hope of Christ, we are not easily shaken. We do not despair when challenges arise. We do not live in fear of the unknown. We walk in confidence, knowing that our future is secure, our purpose is set, our foundation is firm.

There will be days when hope feels hard to hold onto. When doubt whispers that nothing will change, when discouragement tries to settle in. In those moments, we must return to truth. We must remind our hearts that hope is not a feeling—it is a choice. We choose to trust in God's promises, to stand on His Word, to believe that His plans for us are good.

Worship is one of the most powerful ways to cultivate hope. When we lift our voices in praise, even when circumstances seem bleak, we declare that our hope is not in what we see but in who God is. Worship shifts our focus, lifting our eyes above our struggles and fixing them on the One who holds all things together.

Prayer strengthens our hope. When we bring our fears, our doubts, our uncertainties before God, we are reminded that we do not carry them alone. He invites us to cast our burdens upon Him, to lay down every worry, to step into His presence and receive the peace that comes from trusting Him completely.

God's Word fuels our hope. Every promise, every testimony, every reminder of His faithfulness throughout history reassures us that He has not changed. The same God who led His people through the wilderness, who calmed the storm with a word, who raised the dead to life—that same God is with us now.

Hope is not about ignoring reality. It is not about pretending that life is easy or that struggles do not exist. It is about believing that even in the struggle, God is working. It is about trusting that His plans are greater than our own. It is about holding onto the truth that what we see now is not the end of the story.

Paul's prayer is that we would be filled with joy and peace *as we trust in Him.* This is the key. Hope flourishes in the soil of trust. The more we surrender, the more we rest in God's hands, the more we release our need to control—we find ourselves filled with a hope that does not waver.

Perhaps today, you are in need of renewed hope. Maybe life has worn you down, and the weight of waiting has made you feel weary. If that is you, take heart. The God of hope is near. He is not distant. He sees you, He knows you, and He is at work in ways you cannot yet see.

You were not created to live in despair. You were made to live in hope—unshaken, unwavering, deeply rooted in the One who holds all things together. Let His joy fill you, let His peace cover you, and let His Spirit cause hope to rise within you once again.

**Prayer**

Father, You are the God of hope, the source of all joy and peace. When life feels uncertain, when the waiting is long, when discouragement tries to settle in, help me to fix my eyes on You. Fill me with a hope that is unshaken, a faith that does not waver, a trust that stands firm no matter what comes.

Teach me to rest in Your promises, to believe that You are working even when I cannot see it. Let Your Holy Spirit fill me with overflowing hope, so that my heart is steadfast and my spirit is strong. When fear tries to creep in, remind me that You are greater. When doubt whispers, let Your truth be louder.

I surrender every worry, every unanswered question, every burden into Your hands. I choose to trust You, to walk in joy, to live in peace, knowing that my hope is secure in You. Thank You for being faithful, for never leaving me, for leading me into a future filled with purpose and promise. In Jesus' name, Amen.

**Faith-Building Action Step**

Take a moment today to reflect on God's faithfulness in your life. Write down a time when He answered a prayer, provided in a way you did not expect, or carried you through a difficult season. Let that testimony be a reminder that He is still at work, still writing your story. Each time you feel discouraged, return to this truth—your hope is unshaken because it is placed in the hands of a faithful God.

# 36

# Conclusion

Y ou did it. You have walked through 30 days of faith, reflection, and transformation. Through the highs and the lows, the challenges and the victories, you have taken steps to draw closer to God, to release your anxieties into His hands, and to strengthen your trust in His perfect plan. You have spent time in His presence, meditating on His promises, and allowing His truth to shape your heart.

But this is not the end of your journey. It is only the beginning. What God has started in you through this devotional is meant to continue beyond these pages, leading you into deeper intimacy with Him, unwavering trust, and an enduring hope that remains unshaken through every season of life.

*Reflecting on the 30-Day Journey*

Over these past 30 days, you have explored what it means to trust God in uncertainty, to surrender your worries, to stand firm in faith, and to walk in unshaken hope. You have learned to cast your cares on the Lord, to worship through the storm, to embrace His perfect peace, and to see trials as opportunities for growth.

Each day, as you opened your heart to God's Word, He was working—shaping, healing, and strengthening you. Perhaps you have experienced moments of deep revelation, times when His presence felt undeniable. Or maybe your growth has been more subtle, like a steady unfolding of peace and confidence. Whatever your experience has been, know this: every moment spent seeking Him was not wasted. Every time you lifted your heart in prayer, every Scripture you meditated on, every faith-building step you took—God saw it, and He is using it to mold you into the person He created you to be.

God has begun a good work in you, and He will be faithful to complete it (Philippians 1:6). The truths you have encountered in this devotional are not just for these 30 days—they are meant to be carried with you for a lifetime, woven into your daily life, and used as a foundation for your continued journey of faith.

## Continuing to Trust God Beyond This Devotional

Spiritual growth does not end here. Just as a tree does not stop growing once it takes root, your faith is meant to deepen, expand, and flourish. God's Word is living and active, always speaking new truths into your heart. Continue to meditate on Scripture, to seek Him in prayer, and to cultivate a life that is centered on faith. The more you immerse yourself in His truth, the more His peace, strength, and presence will guide you.

As you move forward, keep these practices close:

- **Stay in God's Word.** The Bible is your foundation. Let it guide your steps, comfort your heart, and renew your mind. Make daily Scripture reading a habit that nourishes your soul.
- **Pray without ceasing.** Keep the conversation with God open. He delights in hearing from you, in sharing your burdens, and in revealing His plans to you.
- **Surround yourself with faith-filled community.** Whether it's a church, a small group, or trusted friends, find people who will encourage and uplift you in your walk with Christ. You were never meant to do this alone.
- **Live out your faith daily.** Faith is not just something we believe—it's something we live. Show God's love in your words, actions, and interactions with others. Let your life be a reflection of the transformation He is working in you.
- **Hold onto hope, even in the waiting.** There will be days when you don't feel strong, when fear tries to creep in, when you wonder if God is still near. Keep trusting, keep praying, and keep pressing forward. God is always working, even when you cannot yet see it.

Remember, faith is a journey, not a destination. Some days will be easier than others, but God is always with you, guiding you, strengthening you, and reminding you that He is your unshaken hope.

*Encouraging Others with Your Testimony*

Your story matters. What God has done in your life over these past 30 days is not just for you—it is meant to be shared. Whether you have found peace in a storm, a renewed sense of trust, or a deeper relationship with Him, your testimony has the power to inspire and uplift others.

Consider sharing what God has done in your life:

- **With a friend who is struggling.** Your words could be the encouragement they need.
- **In a journal, as a personal record of God's faithfulness.** Writing down what you have learned will remind you of His goodness in future seasons. As you look back, you will see how far He has brought you.
- **On social media or in conversations.** Your testimony may be the light someone else needs to see.
- **In your community.** Whether through church, small groups, or online faith communities, your story could encourage someone to begin their own journey of trust and hope.

You never know how God may use your words to plant a seed in someone's heart. Your journey may be the spark that leads someone else to seek Him more deeply.

*Closing Words of Gratitude & Next Steps*

Thank you for taking this journey. Thank you for showing up each day, for opening your heart, and for trusting God with your fears and uncertainties. It is my deepest prayer that *Hope Unshaken* has strengthened you, encouraged you, and reminded you that no matter what happens in life, God is always in control.

But this is just the beginning. God has so much more in store for you. Keep pressing forward. Keep seeking Him. Keep choosing faith over fear, hope over despair, and trust over doubt. He is faithful, and He will never leave you.

If this devotional has blessed you, I invite you to share it with others who may need encouragement. One of the best ways you can help spread this message of faith and hope is by leaving a review on Amazon. Your words could be the reason someone else picks up this devotional and begins their own journey of transformation.

Most of all, never forget: you are loved, you are seen, and you are never alone. The same God who walked with you through these 30 days walks with you every day of your life. Keep trusting, keep believing, and keep walking forward in the unshaken hope that is found in Him alone.

With faith and gratitude,
 **Elijah Carter**

Made in the USA
Columbia, SC
26 May 2025

58461651R00098